Praise for

OUT OF THE STORM AND INTO GOD'S ARMS

While our world has no shortage of bad things, it does have a shortage of answers to why bad things happen to good people. In *Out of the Storm and into God's Arms*, the ancient book of Job comes alive with relevant answers to difficult questions about suffering—bringing personal comfort, giving permanent hope, lifting us to a higher dimension of faith in a loving God.

Anne Graham Lotz, international Bible teacher
and author of *Just Give Me Jesus*

I must have a case of Job-i-tis because last week felt like a month of stormy days. Thank you, Jill, for reminding me that as long as there is breath in my body, there will be hardship—and hope. Your stories stirred my emotions, and your insights on Job have inspired me to face my storms with greater spiritual clarity and dexterity.

Patsy Clairmont, author of *God Uses Cracked Pots*
and *Stardust on My Pillow*

As a mother, career woman and youth pastor's wife, sometimes I feel as if I'm enduring a number of storms! Jill Briscoe has given us a glimpse of God's joy through the sorrow and peace within pain. A delightful, useful silver lining for anyone walking through cloudy days.

Angela Elwell Hunt, author of *Loving Someone Else's Child!*
and *The Tale of Three Trees*

With clarity Jill Briscoe relates the events in Job to you and me, and with warmth and understanding she connects Job, his friends, his family, and our God to each of us. *Out of the Storm and into God's Arms* is a handbook for anyone who is enduring hardship, be it great or small.

Lynn Morris, coauthor of *Shadows of the Mountains* and *The Stars for a Light*

In her personal and warm style, Jill Briscoe gives an uplifting perspective to help us face our unexplainable sorrows and struggles. She offers refreshing insight to help us apply to our everyday lives the wonderful lessons she uncovers in the story of Job. This is a book for everyone who asks, "Why?" and finds there are few answers. Jill reminds us that where the good news is, there is victory. Jill's openness and vulnerability are indicative of her life and ministry, and it helps me to know that her walk with God has similar struggles to my own. She has always been a personal role model for me, and I continue to thank God for bringing her gifts and heart across our paths.

Mary Whelchel, founder of the Christian Working Woman radio ministry

Jill has done it again. This book is solidly biblical, is practical in its application, captures the mind of the reader and convincingly demonstrates the faithfulness of God to bring joy out of suffering.

Nell Maxwell, founder and president Women Alive Canada, Inc.

Out of the *Storm* and into **God's** arms

Shelter in Turbulent Times

JILL BRISCOE

CLC
PUBLICATIONS

Out of the Storm and into God's Arms
Published by CLC Publications

U.S.A.
P.O. Box 1449, Fort Washington, PA 19034

UNITED KINGDOM
CLC International (UK)
Unit 5, Glendale Avenue, Sandycroft, Flintshire, CH5 2QP

Printed in the United States of America

This edition 2017

ISBN-13 (paperback): 978-1-61958-008-4
ISBN-13 (e-book): 978-1-61958-021-3

I dedicate this book to Job and his daughters—family and friends around the world—who have shown me the way to be up when I'm down.

These are the people who have demonstrated that our faith in Christ as Savior is not misplaced and have testified against all odds that He is there and adequate however black the night, strong the wind or cruel the ways of evil in this our Father's world.

CONTENTS

Introduction 9

1. Gold Faith 11

2. A World Gone Mad 21

3. Accepting the Unacceptable 31

4. Trusting through Trouble 43

5. When Feelings Fail You 55

6. Waiting it Out 67

7. How to Comfort Job 83

8. How to Handle Criticism 93

9. Somebody's Praying for Me 109

10. Persisting through Pain 125

11. Out of the Storm and into His Arms 139

12. Planning to Be Part of His Plan 151

13. Finding the Heart to Forgive 165

14. Job's Daughters 179

15. Finishing Strong 191

    Notes 207

# Introduction

THE world has not changed since I wrote the first edition of this book. The storms of suffering and sorrow continue to storm. The pain in this hurting world continues unabated. But "God is our refuge and strength, an ever-present help in trouble" (Ps. 46:1). His arms are underneath and all around "those who fly to their sheltering." Close to the Father's heart there is peace.

CHAPTER ONE

GOLD FAITH

When he has tested me, I will come forth as gold.

JOB 23:10

In this you greatly rejoice, though now for a little while you may have had to suffer grief in all kinds of trials. These have come so that your faith—of greater worth than gold, which perishes even though refined by fire—may be proved genuine and may result in praise, glory and honor when Jesus Christ is revealed.

1 PETER 1:6–7

PACING up and down at the back of the church in Croatia, my heart racing, I felt something close to panic tighten around my heart as I viewed the people I had been invited to come and "teach."

They had been through the fires of affliction along the Serbian border. Having just arrived in a safe haven, many were in a state of shock. Some had seen their husbands' or sons' throats cut, daughters torn away from them, crammed into trucks and driven out of sight. Others came to our meetings from boxcars they shared with dozens of other displaced people. These temporary accommodations would turn into semipermanent "residences." Still others had on their minds family homes that had been taken over by the enemy. Strangers slept in their beds, wore their clothes, sat at their tables and sifted through their private papers and photographs.

I had come to speak to these afflicted, harassed people. I looked at my notes, carefully and prayerfully prepared, and decided to scrap them! What could I say to these people? What right had I to offer anything, coming to them for a temporary visit from far away, in my own clothing with my stomach full? Our family lived in a safe home that was protected by an efficient police force. Somehow, "God loves you and I do too" sounded a little inadequate.

What would you have said if you had been invited to speak to those people? To which part of the Bible would you have turned? Where can we turn if we are to understand the mystery of suffering? One place in the Scriptures I have visited again and again, not only to find help for myself in difficult times but to find help for others, is the book of Job. During those days in Croatia, I shared this man's story many times.

Job is a beautiful, poetic book, one that scholars continue to mine for jewels of wisdom and insight. We find in this one story the many questions we all ask when disaster strikes, when the worst has happened, when our hope is gone and our vision of the future has dimmed.

Job was one of God's favorite people—did you know that? In the beginning of the book, God's pleasure in this man is clearly expressed. But being in God's favor didn't prevent Job's life from falling apart. How did he cope? Why did God allow such awful things to happen to one of His own—to one of His best? The book of Job doesn't answer all the questions about suffering that our bewildered hearts ask, but it does answer the questions some of us never ask and ought to be asking!

THE WORLD THAT BROKE GOD'S HEART

As I have traveled this world from east to west and have seen God's fingerprints in His marvelous creation, I have had to conclude that *this is God's world!* As I have looked with awe and delight at His creative handiwork on all continents, I could almost hear Him say to me as He said to Job:

Where were you when I laid the earth's foundation? Tell me, if you understand. Who marked off its dimensions? Surely you know! Who stretched a measuring line across it? On what were its footings set, or who laid its cornerstone—while the morning stars sang together and all the angels shouted for joy? (Job 38:4–7)

Yes, this is my Father's world. Yet the pain and evil I have seen help me to understand a little bit better why this, my Father's world, broke my Father's heart. I understand in a new way why it says in Genesis 6:5–6, "The LORD saw how great man's wickedness on the earth had become, and that every inclination of the thoughts of his heart was only evil all the time. The LORD was grieved that he had made man on the earth, and his heart was filled with pain."

I have visited prisoners in Taiwan, stood in the killing fields of Cambodia, heard a bomb blast close at hand in Croatia, watched British SWAT teams hunt for terrorists in Northern Ireland, and returned home to the "good old US of A" to hear of hundreds of our own kids killing each other on the streets. As I look and listen in all these situations, the violence, the victimization, as well as the victory of the book of Job begin to make sense to me. There is so much pain, not only in our extreme physical dilemmas but also in the emotional and relational realms. Husbands and wives beat and devour each other; children agonize over what they did wrong to cause Daddy or Mommy to leave the family; mental and verbal abuse are meted out to tiny children, the old and the infirm. Even churches and some of their leaders self-destruct, bringing spiritual pain to hundreds of disillusioned people.

But I am a Christian. And so I believe that this, my Father's world that broke my Father's heart, has not been abandoned. This is God's world, and he wants it back! He will not allow it to blow itself to pieces. As Job puts it, "I know that you can do all things; no plan of yours can be thwarted" (Job 42:2). God *does* have a plan—a purpose for this hurting world. It is to reconcile people to Himself through Christ, to give humanity a chance to know Him, to be forgiven, and to learn how to forgive in return. Our heavenly Father wants us to live empowered by Him in this life, with the certain hope of living with Him in glory in the next. To this end, the Father calls individuals to Himself and makes them a family, entrusting His own to make this good news known to those who have never heard it.

What We Have in Common with Job— and with Jesus

As I have traveled this broken world, I have met my Father's family. And I have seen Job's story—its pain, its lessons and its triumph—reenacted time and time again. I've known missionaries and nationals who have believed the good news and who are out there with their children in difficult and often dangerous places. Some of them live in accommodations where they catch twenty rats a week! They work with widows, orphans, the maimed, the halt and the blind. They give help and encouragement to refugees, the poorest of the poor, displaced people, squatter dwellers and young delinquents. Others reach the I-have-need-of-nothing group: wealthy people who experience an intimate loneliness that nothing can fill.

Not only have I seen God's fingerprints in His creation, I have seen His footprints in the lives of His people, God's forever family. They are bearing testimony to the saving power of the living Christ. They are bright lights in dark places and "salt of the earth" that preserves rather than corrupts. All of them are saying loudly and clearly to their world, as Job said to his, "I know that my Redeemer lives!"

These people are telling their world that God has visited them in their pain. They are responding rightly to suffering, which is, after all, part and parcel of life lived with a sinful nature in a fallen environment. These people are saying with Job, "He knows the way that I take; when he has tested me, I will come forth as gold" (23:10). There is, however, no gold without the fires of affliction.

I think of my bridesmaid—an Irish beauty, whom I met when she was fifteen, agonizing over the slow death of her mother. An only child and yet still a child herself, she grieved deeply. Yet she put her teenage hand into her heavenly Father's and walked through the flames. The day of her mother's funeral, she gave me a poem that told me her heart.

> I am leading my child to the heavenly land.
> I am guiding her day by day,
> and I ask her now as I take her hand
> to come home by a rugged way.
> It is not a way she herself would choose,
> for its beauty she cannot see.
> But she knows not what her soul would lose
> if she trod not this path with me.
>
> —Anonymous

Ann is one of Job's daughters. She has been married to a Belfast policeman during all the troubles in Northern Ireland, with plenty of opportunities to practice her faith!

And then, of course, there are my Croatian friends, the "Jobs" I mentioned at the beginning of this chapter. What can I say of them? What did I finally decide to say to them?

If only I had suffered more, I thought, *then I would have something to say.* Yet I had not come in my own name with my own words. I knew I was an ambassador for Christ, who had suffered. I had been invited by these people to bring a word from my King about His heart and His kingdom—a kingdom where one day there would be no more pain or sorrow and where all tears would be wiped away. Walking up the steps to the pulpit and looking at those faces, I prayed I would truly represent the One who had sent me.

The words came then, swiftly, the interpreter's voice hardly interrupting the flow. I told them, "Jesus' parents had to escape murderous soldiers who tried to kill their baby. They fled in the night with their precious little boy who was barely two years old. They became refugees in Egypt, a foreign land." Eyes brightened in the pews. Arms of parents, grandparents, aunts and uncles, tightened around their precious children, and they paid close attention. The Holy Spirit gave me more gentle words. I told them Jesus had a big family. He was poor, by trade a craftsman. His father died, and He cared for a widowed mother and many sisters and brothers. He worked hard. But there came a day when He had to leave His home and let others care for His family. That must have been very difficult for Him. Heads nodded. These people understood such loss of control.

"Jesus knew what it was to be homeless," I continued. "One day He said, 'Foxes have dens and birds have nests, but I, the Messiah, have no home of My own—no place to lay My head.' Sometimes He was hungry; sometimes He was thirsty. Sometimes He didn't have time to sleep—even under the stars! Then one day, evil men hammered Him to a cross—naked. He was tortured, and yet He forgave His tormentors. He was cursed, yet He prayed for those who cursed Him. He was rejected and abandoned by His friends, but He didn't hold it against them, and He died of his terrible wounds and a broken heart."

Tears began to fall down these worn faces, etched with grief. It was very quiet in the church. I went on to apply the truth I was telling.

"Some of the things that happened to Christ have happened to you. You could not avoid them, You could not stop them from happpening. Pain and sorrow have come, and you could not escape them. You have had no choice in the matter. But *this* Jesus—this King—this One sent from heaven, had a choice! He did not need to be treated in such a way. What's more, He knew before He came what He was in for. He was God, and so He had power to resist, to hit back, to get even. He had the power to save Himself. Yet He chose not to. Why? He had a reason, a purpose for allowing Himself to be crucified: He loved us. He came to us in our terrible world and experienced our trials, our problems and our pain. He died in order to forgive us and reconcile us to God and to each other."

A hymn began quietly. Some men and women stood; others knelt, lifting their hands toward God. Many wept openly. Then the meeting was over, and we went out to the medical, feeding and clothing distribution centers—the day's work had only begun.

When trouble comes, it's important to ask the right person the right questions. God is shown in the book of Job as not only accessible but also greater than Satan and stronger than the sin that so easily besets us. God is able to sustain and supply His own people when trouble comes. When we learn how to turn to God and ask the important questions, we will hear the answers loud and clear—and in the hearing "find grace to help us in our times of need" (Heb. 4:16, TLB).

As we meet Job and his children, present-day people who have found the secret of peace in the midst of their pain and tranquility in their confusion, let's learn from their example and know in reality that "when He has tried us, we will come forth as gold."

What Does It Mean?

The questions at the end of each chapter can be used for personal or group study. If you are part of a group studying this book, choose someone at each session to lead the group through the questions and prayer suggestions at the end of each chapter. If you are studying on your own, record your thoughts and discoveries in a notebook or journal.

1. The Bible says God was sorry He had made us (Gen. 6:6). Does this shock you? Why or why not? Do you think we take the grace of God for granted? If so, give an example of how we do this.

2. Read Job 1:13–22. What are your thoughts on Job's response to these disasters in verse 20?

3. Read Job 19:25–27. Make a list from these verses of all the things Job knew about the Lord. What does "I know that my Redeemer lives" mean to you?

4. Job believed in the one true God. What can we gather about the religion of others around him from Job 31:26–28?

5. So many people believe that humanity is improving all the time. What does the Bible say about the human heart in Genesis 6:5–6? in Psalm 14:1–3? What needs to happen to our hearts according to Second Corinthians 4:6? In Ezekiel 36:26 what did God promise to give us?

6. Read Job 1:21, Ecclesiastes 7:14 and Ruth 1:21, and consider: what did Solomon and Naomi have in common with Job?

7. Today, if disaster strikes, what kind of help can we get? What help do you think Job had available to him, if any?

How Should I Pray?

- Pray for all the people you know who need a new start.

- Pray for people who are enjoying good times—that they will use their blessings wisely and get to know God thoroughly.

- Pray for those who are enduring hard times—that they will not charge God with wrongdoing.

- Pray for the many Jobs in this world who are "on their own."

- Praise God for the different kinds of support we enjoy.

CHAPTER TWO

A WORLD GONE MAD

*There is no one on earth like him; he is blameless and upright,
a man who fears God and shuns evil.*

JOB 1:8

*Remember those earlier days after you had received the light, when you stood
your ground in a great contest in the face of suffering. Sometimes you were
publicly exposed to insult and persecution; at other times you stood side by
side with those who were so treated. You sympathized with those in prison
and joyfully accepted the confiscation of your property because you knew
that you yourselves had better and lasting possessions.*

HEBREWS 10:32–34

WE don't find the book of Job until right before Psalms—near the middle of the Bible. But it is actually one of the oldest books of the Bible. Records of Uz, the shadowy land that was Job's home, predate written records of Hebrew law. We are talking about a book that is pre-Abraham, pre-Hebrews, pre-Moses, "pre-" almost everything! Yet Job calls God El Shaddai thirty-one times. El Shaddai means "comforter, supplier, the meeter of our needs," and Job, as we shall see, had a lot of needs to be met.

Job believed in the God we believe in. This is amazing, since people around him believed in many gods; it was a polytheistic environment. By believing in one God, Job created his own monotheistic culture. In chapter 31:26–28 he refers to the worship of the sun and moon and says, "If I have looked at the sun shining in the skies, or the moon walking down her silver pathway, and my heart has been secretly enticed, and I have worshiped them by kissing my hand to them, this, too, must be punished by the judges. For if I had done such things, it would mean that I denied the God of heaven" (TLB). Before the one true God ever appeared to Moses, he appeared to Job and to his friends, Eliphaz, Bildad, Zophar and Elihu. It is a mistake to think that the knowledge of the one true God was restricted to Abraham and his descendants. Even though idolatry abounded, there were pockets of true religion in the early civilization of which Job was a part.

It's amazing to me that Job knew so much about so much! For example, he tells us, "I know that my Redeemer lives" (Job 19:25). He believed in a living Redeemer. In the opening verses of the book, God calls Job "righteous" (meaning that Job was made right with God), "blameless" (not perfect, but forgiven), "a man who fears God and shuns evil" (1:8). He was a completely sincere and godly man with no secrets to cover up! He was also a force to be reckoned with in his community. "He was, in fact, the richest cattleman in that entire area" (1:3, TLB). As is so often the case, Job's reputation was linked to how well he had handled his wealth and position. He lived at the beginning of time, pitting his wits against the wild frontier of early civilization.

Yet even though he was a good man who loved God and treated his neighbors fairly, Job was not exempt from suffering. The book of Job teaches us, among other things, that suffering is part and parcel of the universal experience of life on this planet—life in a fallen environment lived by people with a fallen nature. But Job responded to his suffering in such a way that he delighted the very heart of God. Morris A. Inch, in *My Servant Job*, says,

We learn more from God's excited estimate of this sage [Job] than from man's dour explorations into his torments. We will want also to look over the Almighty's shoulder, to see where His finger points, to appreciate what provoked His enthusiasm, to benefit from His direction.[1]

What happened to Job has to do with the hard things we all face—not only those things we bring on ourselves or perpetrate on others, but also senseless evil, the suffering of the innocent, and "acts of God." Above all, Job's story explores the suffering that is permitted to come to the person who genuinely and purposefully loves God.

A Hole in the Hedge

Job seems to have lived a charmed life. God had "put a hedge" around the man and all that belonged to him. How do we know that? The devil tells us! Now that's a shock! Right at the beginning of the story, in Job chapter 1, we are given a peep into another world. The Lord Almighty is holding court, and the angels are giving an account of themselves to him. Satan, our enemy—the accuser of all believers—appears. Satan had stolen the hearts of people and made them his own, until their every inclination was "only evil all the time" (Gen. 6:5). Sin had affected everything—even nature itself—and God's world had become a place where "they loved the darkness more than the Light, for their deeds were evil" (John 3:19, TLB). But this is God's world, and God wants it back. Here and there, God draws men and women to himself and uses them in his plan of redemption. People like Job.

We see, here at the beginning of Job's story, that the devil also has a plan. He had been an angel called "Lucifer, son of the morning"; because of his rebellion, he is now a devil called "Satan, father of the night." He complains that Job is pampered and spoiled. He, Satan, has been prevented from tempting this man, and he suggests that if he had the opportunity to reach him, Job would soon curse God to his face (Job 1:11). "Why shouldn't Job return the favor when You bribe him with gifts?" he says, in effect. "You have guarded all he owns, never letting any tiny trouble touch him. Just look how rich You've helped him to become. No wonder he thinks You're so great! But just take away his wealth, and You'll see what he thinks of You!" Knowing that temptation is not only a chance to do wrong but also an opportunity to do right and so grow in character and grace, the Lord gives Satan permission to tempt Job. Yet the permission has boundaries. "You may do anything you like with his wealth," he is told, "but don't harm him physically" (1:12, TLB). Now a hole has been allowed to appear in the heavenly hedge—a divinely permitted hole.

So there came a day when Job awoke to a world gone mad, his world. He would never be the same again. God had directed Satan to contemplate Job's life and behavior. The Lord had boasted about his servant: "There is no one on earth like him" (1:8). When I first read this, it made me a little uncomfortable. *Perhaps if I lived a life that really pleased God*, I thought, *He might point it out to Satan and say, "Have you ever considered my servant Jill?"*! This idea leads me to wonder if it's safe to be so good! I don't feel that I need the attention of that evil creature, Satan, drawn to me; I have enough troubles as it is.

However, I am comforted to see that God's affirmation of Job's righteous character did not allow Satan any special privileges. Satan—the source of all evil—operates under the sovereign power of a God who will permit him only limited freedom. Satan is still, in a sense, God's servant. We must never forget that Satan does not belong in the same echelon of the spirit world in which God dwells. God is God, and He alone occupies that position. Satan belongs to the sphere of created beings called angels, and the created creature never possesses the place or power of the Creator. Satan cannot, without our acquiescence, destroy the person God has made us to be, but he is sometimes allowed to take the things we have accumulated.

Job's worst nightmare happened all in a day. It was a "daymare." It had to have been a Monday! All in a day he lost his cattle and all his wealth. He and his flocks became victims of the violence of terrorism. A storm hit, the lightning struck Job's animals and servants, and burned up his barns and cattle sheds. But worst of all, a tornado hit the house where his ten children were having a party, and his seven sons and three daughters died—all in a day! (1:13–19).

When Trials Touch Those We Love

The "everything" that Satan was permitted to touch included Job's precious children. Possessions are one thing, but people are quite another—especially people whom we love very much. As Henry Gariepy says in his excellent book about Job, *Portraits of Perseverance*,

> We will not only have our own problems. The problems of those we love and care for and for whom we have such high hopes and dreams, hit us with full force as well. When tragedy strikes them, the quakes in their lives are registered on the Richter Scale of our own hearts.[2]

I know that in my own experience I do a halfway decent job of trusting the Lord until something touches one of our children. In a way, our children are my Achilles heel, and Satan knows it! I have always worried about the kids. When they were little, I worried that they would fall into the washing machine and drown. When they were teenagers, I worried about the friendships they made. When they went away to college, I worried about the life partners they would choose. When none of my worries materialized (and it has been said that 90 percent of our worries and fears never do), I began to worry all over again about their children falling into the washing machine and drowning—and so on! Like Job, I pray fervently for them, but I have seldom been free from the "dread" Job experienced and testifies to in chapter 3:25–26. Only recently has God released me from this fear. Partly, the acceptance of the fact that trouble, in some measure, will come, has helped. But more importantly, peace has grown out of the conviction that *when*, not *if*, trouble comes, God will Himself be all that my children need in order to cope.

An Unlikely Response

Job, incredibly, does not declare war on God when disaster comes but rather responds in worship. That's right—in worship! "The Lord gave me everything I had, and they were his to take away. Blessed be the name of the Lord" (1:21, TLB). It may strike you as a little weird that someone could lose everything he owns, as well as all his children, and say, "Praise the Lord," but we need to look a little bit closer to get the real impact of Job's amazing response. His trouble is the same trouble that comes to all of us, the just and the unjust, because of that original sin in the Garden of Eden. Job had actually wondered why God had kept the inevitable results of the Fall from visiting him for so long! He had been waiting for the sky to fall on his head for a long time: "What I always feared has happened to me. I was not fat and lazy, yet trouble struck me down" (3:25–26, TLB).

Some commentators believe Job had lived at least seventy years in peace and tranquility up to this point. But even though he resided in a wild environment, among roving bands of cattle thieves and vagabonds, when trouble first came to Job, he did not ask why, but rather, why not—because he knew trouble was to be expected. He understood that the Lord may well give, or the Lord may well take away. In accepting this Job found a measure of peace when trouble eventually came, and he refused to charge God with wrongdoing. He would not interpret this trouble as proof of a flaw in God's perfect nature. He insisted that God is a holy God and has a perfect right to give or to withhold His blessings and protection. And so Job passed his first test with flying colors.

A "Job" in Northern Ireland

Some years ago Bill met us at Belfast Airport in Northern Ireland. He was a well-known businessman in that troubled city. My husband, Stuart, and I were conducting some meetings for the YMCA, and even though security was tight (you had to check your car for bombs if it was parked in certain places, and you were searched when you went into a store), night after night the downtown auditorium filled with young people.

The last evening came too quickly, and we went to a restaurant to eat with our friends before leaving. We had just finished the first course when the police arrived to tell Bill that the building where he had his offices had been bombed. "The IRA claimed it," the officer said. "They told us they used forty bombs. There's not much left, I'm afraid."

We went to see, and sure enough, there wasn't much left. We walked up the blackened stairs, watching firemen do their work and tenants of other office suites sift through debris, trying to rescue records or machines. All the fire alarms were ringing, and I wondered if anyone knew how many of the forty bombs the IRA claimed to have planted had exploded!

We watched our friend as he talked to a police officer who knew him. The man was a Christian and was promising to stay on late into the night and help Bill salvage things. "No, no," Bill said, thanking him. "Tomorrow is the Lord's Day, and we need to be ready to worship Him." Like Job, Bill was able to say, "The Lord gave me everything I had, and they were his to take away. Blessed be the name of the Lord." This particular modern Job was able to take "the spoiling of [his] goods" cheerfully (Heb. 10:34, KJV). He too passed his test with flying colors.

But the story of Job was just getting started. Another dreadful day was on its way. In the biblical narrative the scene shifts back to the courts of heaven. Satan is again constrained to give an account of his deadly patrol. Once more God affirms the godly character of His servant Job. This time Satan points out why he thinks Job's victory is a hollow one: "Skin for skin. A man will give anything to save his life. Touch his body with sickness, and he will curse you to your face!" "Do with him as you please," the Lord replies, "only spare his life." So, the Scriptures tell us, "Satan went out from the presence of the Lord and struck Job with a terrible case of boils from head to foot. Then Job took a broken piece of pottery to scrape himself, and sat among the ashes" (2:4–8, TLB). And then along came his wife!

What Does It Mean?

1. Read Job 1:1–5, 8. What can we learn from God about Job?

2. Read Job 31. In this chapter Job defends his integrity. What can we learn from Job about Job? Does he sound as if he is bragging? Explain your answer. Which of his statements in this passage challenges you the most?

3. God is well aware of who we are and what we are doing. Job 31:4 says, "Does he not see my ways and count my every step?" What do you think God would have said to

Satan about you if you, and not Job, were the object of a heavenly debate? Would it have been complimentary?

4.   Read Job 31 again. The whole chapter has to do with Job's relationships with other people. Write the verse that shows Job's integrity in his dealings with the following:

- his wife

- his servants

- the poor

- his money

- godless philosophy

- his enemy

- strangers

How Should I Pray?

- Pray that we may be people of Christian integrity like Job.

- Pray for leaders who have fallen in moral matters and need restoring to faith and fellowship.

- Pray about your own integrity in your relationships with those listed under question 4.

- Pray for your leaders' lives and witness in all of these areas.

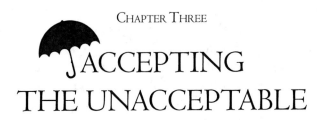

CHAPTER THREE

ʃACCEPTING THE UNACCEPTABLE

Shall we accept good from God, and not trouble?

JOB 2:10

*Every good and perfect gift is from above, coming down
from the Father of the heavenly lights, who does not change
like shifting shadows.*

JAMES 1:17

I WAS a small child during World War II. As the war wound to a close and news began to filter out that thousands of people had been put to death in the Nazi concentration camps, I remember asking my mother, "Who are the Jews?" "They are God's people," she replied.

"I'm glad I'm not one of them," I said. It struck me that if that was how God neglected His own, there appeared to be no real advantage to belonging to Him!

This viewpoint is well represented in the story of Job and particularly in the attitude of Job's wife. When Satan took everything he could from Job, he decided to leave him his wife. Perhaps the devil thought she would be a great help to his cause! It appears that she didn't respond as well as her husband did to the trouble that came to them. We must remember, however, that Job's wife was suffering too. She had lost everything that Job had lost. She had lost her children—all ten of them—and all in a day's time. Yet the greatest loss for Job's wife was the loss of her faith in the integrity of God and His ability to sustain His people. I have to admit that I see myself more readily responding to trials as Job's wife did than as Job did.

In her opinion God was to be roundly criticized, even condemned, for allowing all this trouble to happen to her wonderful husband. After all, everyone knew what a marvelous man Job was and what an exemplary life he had lived. Why had God allowed these catastrophes to happen to one of His choice servants?

As poor Job was afflicted with "a terrible case of boils from head to foot" and sat among ashes, scraping himself with a piece of pottery, his wife said to him, "Are you still trying to be godly when God has done all this to you? Curse him and die" (2:7–9, TLB).

Job's wife's advice was short and to the point: Curse God and die. To her it was perfectly logical to blame God. And since God had been so neglectful in His care and provision, there was no real reason to go on living. "Why don't you commit suicide?" she suggested. Job rebuked her for talking like a "heathen [unbelieving] woman." She was not an unbeliever, just talking like one! Job reminded his wife that when trouble arrives on the doorstep, we need to respond as believers and not as unbelievers. "Shall we accept good from God, and not trouble?" he asked her (2:10).

PRAISE PREPARES US FOR PROBLEMS

Learning to receive the good gifts of God, praising Him and cultivating a thankful attitude in general, gets us into the right frame of mind to accept the problems of life. Job and his family had been the recipients of God's free blessings for seventy years. Their hands had been open wide, stretched out toward heaven, to receive all the Lord gave them. Job refused to take those same outstretched hands and clench them into fists to shake in the face of God when the gifts of grace, health, wealth and happiness were withheld. After all, the Giver of gifts has a perfect right to give or to withhold. He is under no obligation to us whatsoever. Having been a truly thankful man all his life helped Job when he had nothing to be thankful about. *Praise prepares us for problems.* It doesn't keep trouble away, but it gets us ready for trouble when it comes.

Are you a negative or a positive person? Even if your personality or circumstance leads you to live in the shadows rather than the light, you can begin to discipline yourself to think about the good, not the evil, side of life. Paul enjoins us to do just that. "Fix your thoughts on what is true and good and right. Think about things that are pure and lovely, and dwell on the fine, good things in others. Think about all you can praise God for and be glad about" (Phil. 4:8, TLB).

A dear friend stricken with terminal cancer wrote to me along these very lines. She said, "I have existed in a healthy body for so many years, this is all so new to me. Oh yes, I do clench my fists at times. It's still difficult to accept and understand, since there is no history of cancer in my family and I have practiced all the healthy habits all of these years. But again and again, prayer and thanksgiving bring me back to an understanding and to an 'attitude of gratitude.' I've been blessed in so many ways."

SURPRISED BY GRACE

When we look closely at Job's story, we recognize that Job did not discover significant aspects of God's character until the blessings were withheld. Before Job went through his trials, he knew God as a God of power, wisdom and justice. Until he suffered, he did not know Him as a God of loving grace. Job talks about God's "whisper" (26:14). It is these still, small whispers of comfort in the ears of our souls that explain why it is necessary perhaps to spend some time out of our comfort zone. How would we ever know God to be adequate if we had never been inadequate? How would we ever have our tears wiped away if we had never cried? Job was well aware that the honor and success that had been his were gifts of grace. He had been able to hold his material wealth lightly and not tightly. As David McKenna suggests in *The Whisper of His Grace*, "being right with God" should help us in "doing right with things," so we don't suffer from "affluenza."[1]

Job did not waste needless energy asking why these terrible things happened to him. He immediately began to look for hope and light—without the answers. This mind-set helped him to put the little strength he had left into seeking to be a distinctive believer in the midst of his suffering. He was well aware that others were watching him closely. This is always the case.

I remember when I was a new Christian taking note of how people coped with trouble. The people I knew who claimed to belong to Christ—who were committed Christians—responded differently from those who made no profession of faith at all. This was not lost on me.

There was a man I knew who worked in a factory, a workplace in which there was a strong atheistic element. Even though this man tried to speak about his faith, no one would listen. We knew the family through business and were aware that he and his wife had been trying to have a baby for years.

One day the man's wife got pregnant. They were both ecstatic. The man shared his good news with his workmates, who showed little interest. They showed considerable interest, however, when the child was born with a severe handicap.

"That's funny," commented the hard-bitten union chief. "We don't believe in a god, and our kids are healthy! What sort of a god would give you a handicapped child?"

"What did you say?" I asked our friend, aghast at such a comment.

"I just said, 'I'm so very glad God gave her to us and not to you.'"

I was amazed, and even though a new believer, I took note of the distinctive way God enables His children to handle pain and testify of God's grace in it. There is no doubt in my mind that even though our friend's workmates would rather die than admit it, they too must have been impressed!

FLYING INTO OUR FATHER'S ARMS

A train was rattling along the track from one city to another. It carried a full load, and the journey was a long one. In one car the boredom was alleviated slightly by the entertainment afforded the passengers by a small child who flitted from one person to another, smiling and chattering away. She was a personable and sociable little girl, and the passengers began to wonder who her parents were. It was hard to tell, as she gave her attention to each and every one in turn. The passengers, however, were not left wondering for long. Suddenly the train whistled and entered a long, dark tunnel. The little girl flew across the car, straight into the arms of her father!

When trouble comes, the world needs to see us flying into our Father's arms. People are desperate for that example. We need to show them there is a place to hide when we suddenly enter the long, dark tunnel, and they need to hear from us that the arms we run to are loving ones. *In our refusal to charge God with a spiteful spirit, we publicly profess our belief that God is good.*

I have watched in amazement as an expensively dressed businessman, on the way to his state-of-the-art office in downtown Tokyo, placed a bunch of bananas on the branch of a tree outside his high-rise office building. That bunch of bananas was still there at the end of the day. No one touched them because everyone knew that this was someone's effort to appease the spirits that they believed lived in that particular tree. To believe in gods that wish you harm and that must be appeased by a bunch of bananas seems ludicrous to us, and yet we are in danger of the same attitude ourselves. Even believers—like Job's wife—fall into the trap of believing they didn't give God enough bananas (or money in the church offerings), and that is why trouble came. The God who is revealed in Scripture is not a God who must be pampered and appeased but rather a God of love and hope who promises to be all that we need Him to be, when we need Him.

Nobody knows what is around the corner of tomorrow. But one thing we can know: God will be waiting there for us. He is a God of comfort, a God well-acquainted with grief and suffering, a God who knows what it is to have the forces of hell do their worst. Because God inhabits our future, He is never surprised by the magnitude of the troubles waiting for us. We may be surprised, but our heavenly Father never is. He who is bigger than any catastrophe is fully capable of looking after His children in the midst of catastrophe.

Job believed that the God who waited around the corner of his tomorrow was a good God. He believed that nothing on earth could happen to him without having first come through the loving hands of God, and that if the trial was acceptable to God, then it needed to be acceptable to him!

ACCEPTING WHAT WE CAN'T CHANGE

Some years ago I heard a well-known Christian leader talking about his eldest son, who had a heart condition. The young man was suddenly taken seriously ill at college and was rushed to the hospital. As the parents sped toward the emergency room, the father said to his wife, "Pray hard; maybe God will be good and our boy will live." His wife replied, "Isn't God good if he dies?" That world-renowned Christian leader spoke quietly about the affirmation of faith in God's character and about ways that he was made anew at that moment of personal crisis. "God *is* good," he said to his wife, "whether our boy lives or dies." The boy died, but his parents were able to say with Job, "The Lord gave me everything I had, and they were His to take away. Blessed be the name of the Lord."

When we accept that the "unacceptable" has come to us with the full knowledge and permission of a God of integrity, we can stop trying to push the trouble away. The sooner we can accept what we cannot change, the sooner we are ready to experience the peace and healing that we need.

Most of us have trouble believing "the messenger" when he arrives with bad news. In the story of Job's misfortunes, messenger after messenger arrived, each with a more devastating report than the last. We don't see Job going into a state of denial; he believes what he has been told. I saw this response modeled years ago by a friend of mine.

When we first came to pastor the church in Milwaukee, I had to adjust to the American custom of viewing the body of a person who has died. The first experience I had of this was with a neighbor. She and her husband had been married well over forty years. Both of these dear people had come to faith in Christ soon after we had come to know them and were as fresh and excited about their newfound Savior as little children. Then the husband died. I was introduced to the "viewing" experience the next day and stood with the widow at the side of the casket as relatives and friends filed past.

The sister of the old man was inconsolable. She mourned without hope, standing alongside the widow and murmuring to each guest, "There he is. . . . There he is," as they came past. I shot a look at my new friend to see how she was doing and noticed that she was becoming somewhat agitated. Looking briefly at her husband's corpse, she said to his sister, "If I believed, 'There he is,' I would be of all people most miserable. Do you know what makes this possible instead of impossible for me?"

"No," replied the startled sister.

"There he isn't!" my friend replied with great gusto. "There he isn't—he's with Jesus," she repeated. "Absent from the body— present with the Lord," she concluded. My friend had certain hope of the Resurrection. She knew, without a shadow of a doubt, that she would see her beloved husband again. In accepting death as an inevitable part of life, she began to cope much better than the old man's sister, who couldn't accept the fact that her brother had died. And my friend was just a new believer! She had been able to believe the messenger and accept the sudden death of her husband and, therefore, had been able to be a help to others.

In her book *A Path Through Suffering*, Elisabeth Elliot says, "Suffering, even in its mildest forms—inconvenience, delay, disappointment, discomfort, or anything that is not in harmony with our whims and preferences—we will not tolerate. We even reject and deny it. Stress is the result."[2]

Once when Stuart and I were in the United States and our children were at home in England, our daughter had quite a serious accident. Actually, we had come to Milwaukee to meet the church family who had just called us to leave our home country and minister in America. This involved emigrating from Britain.

We were conducting some youth meetings in a camp up in the beautiful mountains in the Southwest before traveling to Milwaukee when the messenger arrived. My husband came into the cabin and advised me to sit down. "Who's dead?" was my immediate question. "No one," he assured me, "but Judy went through a window and has severed the tendon in her right arm. She's in the hospital!" I was shocked. Where had God been? Why hadn't he taken care of our little girl?

At first I found it difficult to believe the messenger. But decisions had to be made—and at once. Should I, having just arrived, get on the next plane home? I knew we couldn't afford to come back to America again, and we needed to buy the parsonage and finalize the immigration details. I had only one hour to decide what to do, and I prayed that God would help me short-circuit all my angry questions, get over the denial, believe the bad news and accept the trouble for whatever purpose it had been allowed to come into my life. As soon as I had done that, I found myself calm and quite certain as to the course of action I needed to take. After it was over I wrote in my prayer diary that I had learned a valuable lesson. I needed to receive bad news as a sovereign act of a good God's knowledgeable permissive will and in this way diminish the stress that comes with denial and resistance.

There is a legitimate period of denial that has come to be recognized by healthcare professionals as a natural part of the grieving process. While we don't want to disregard this stage (which, in its healthy form, doesn't last long), we can point out that a believer's hope in Christ and in God's working sovereignly in every area of our lives provides an extra resource for dealing with bad news.

Thousands of miles away in a hospital bed, my little girl was learning her own hard lessons. The people she was staying with in our absence told her we couldn't come home. She was lonely and frightened. "It was Dad I wanted," she told me later. "But you know, when I knew he couldn't come and put his arms around me, I asked my heavenly Father to do it instead. And He did! So I know now that when something bad happens and you can't be around, He will be—so it will be all right!" After it was all over I thought about my little "sparrow" with her broken wing and remembered that Jesus never promised that a sparrow would not fall but that a sparrow would never fall without the Father, and I praised Him.

Acceptance Leads to Growth

When I was young, I used to play with caterpillars. There were cute little ones and ugly ones and furry ones and smooth ones. Such variety! But they all had one thing in common: they all formed a chrysalis and spent time becoming a beautiful butterfly. When the time came, the struggle would begin as the little bug fought its way out into the world, a new creature.

One day I saw one little chrysalis jumping around on the tray. I felt so sorry for the little bug inside its "prison," obviously wanting to escape, and I wanted to help. So, running to the house, I found a pair of scissors and carefully cut off the top of the chrysalis to help it out. When the bug popped out, I discovered my mistake. Its wings were deformed, and it was colorless!

How was I to know that the color came into the little thing's wings in the triumph of the struggle? How was I to know that it took that deathly struggle to release the wings in order for that little bug to soar above the earth that had been its natural habitat? When I have been unable to save my children from the hard things in life, I have observed that in the struggle the color of their Christian character has come into their wings, and they have risen above their dire dilemmas.

So it was with Job. He had been a "good" man, but through his tragedies, as we shall see, he became a "gold" one! Whereas the things that he feared had anchored him to the earth, his deathly struggle raised him to a new dimension of living. The Bible calls that victory!

What Does It Mean?

1. Read Job 2:1–10. Do you identify more with Job or his wife? In what ways do believers act as unbelievers ("foolish people") when trouble comes?

2. Write about or share an example of someone who has been a model to you in the way they have responded to suffering. What has helped you to be transformed from a bug into a butterfly?

3. Make a list or share ten things you have to be thankful for. In other words, count your blessings. Make a list or share ten things you take for granted that you should be thankful for. Spend time praising God for everything He has given—and everything He has withheld.

4. Draw up a profile from the following verses about Satan (in some passages he's referred to as "the devil"):

   - Genesis 3:1, 13
   - Matthew 13:39
   - Matthew 25:41
   - Luke 4:2
   - 2 Corinthians 11:3, 14
   - 1 Peter 5:8
   - Revelation 12:9

5. According to Ephesians 4:27, what are the people of God told not to do?

6. According to James 4:7, what are the people of God told to do?

7. Read Job 1:12 and 2:6. What comfort do you get from these verses?

8. Read chapter 3 of Job. Which verses indicate Job was sorry he had ever been born? What is his concept of death in verses 13–15 and 17–19? What does Job tell us in verse 25? Can you identify?

How Should I Pray?

- Pray over the helpful thoughts gleaned from your study.

- Pray that you will resist the devil in the power of the Spirit.

- Pray that others will too.

- Dread could be called "Job's disease." It is a sense of impending disaster and has no place in a Christian's life. Pray that God will release you and others you know from this.

- Meditate on Philippians 4:8.

Chapter Four

TRUSTING THROUGH TROUBLE

Though he slay me, yet will I hope in him.

Job 13:15

I know that through your prayers and the help given by the Spirit of Jesus Christ, what has happened to me will turn out for my deliverance. I eagerly expect and hope that I will in no way be ashamed, but will have sufficient courage so that now as always Christ will be exalted in my body, whether by life or by death.
Philippians 1:19–20

A S we begin to accept that storms happen, and as we meet adversity on a moment-by-moment basis, we are faced with another choice. In what spirit will we accept these dark, difficult days and moments? We can grit our teeth and hunker down to wait out the storm with something akin to fatalism, or we can begin to trust God to bring something good out of a bad situation. Elisabeth Elliot calls this latter approach "a trust that becomes a springboard for action." She delineates a difference between resignation and acceptance—and there is a difference. What is more, Elisabeth Elliot should know!

Doing Something Positive with the Negatives

Along with four other women, Elisabeth waited by a short-wave radio for what must have seemed like an eternity, listening for a message from their husbands, who had taken a flight into hostile Indian territory. The young couples had been trying to reach the Auca Indians in Ecuador with the gospel. When no message was received, a search party was sent out after the men, and eventually the dreadful truth was discovered. The young missionaries were found lying facedown in the river, killed by the poisoned lances of the Indians.

This terrible happening had not been on Elisabeth's agenda! She and her husband, Jim, had been looking forward to a missionary career together. Now her whole world had crashed around her.

Elisabeth discovered she had a choice. She could resign herself to the situation and return home with her young daughter, or she could ask the Lord, "In what redemptive way can you use this?" Elisabeth chose to trust God to do something positive with the negatives. And she decided to be part of the action. She and her young daughter and Rachel Saint (Nate Saint's sister) bravely set off into the jungle and found the tribe that had killed Nate and Jim. The women were well received and allowed to make their home among the Indians. After the Bible was translated and the gospel shared, many in the tribe turned to Christ. Later, Nate and Marge Saint's daughter, Kathie, was baptized in the river where her daddy had died. Truly God used that particular situation in a redemptive way. God wants us to buy up the opportunities that come our way as we learn to trust Him and to use trouble as a springboard for action.

Trusting God brings a certain element of hope to our hearts—a confident expectation that all is not lost and that there is something redeemable in the most awful situation. This trust is a tenacious, spiritual insistence that God can be trusted not only to be totally and thoroughly aware of our dilemmas but also to be in control and already taking eternal measures to work out His ultimate purposes.

"But," you may ask, "what are we supposed to trust God to do for us?" To right the wrong? To reverse a disease? To bring our loved ones back from the dead or an unfaithful spouse home again? Sometimes God does the unbelievable, but other times He doesn't. There are, however, certain things we can bank on His doing.

LEARNING SOMETHING NEW ABOUT GOD

First of all, we can trust God to show us something new about Himself. John 11 tells the story of Lazarus and his two sisters, Mary and Martha, who were close friends of Jesus. One day Lazarus fell ill. Jesus was far away, busy preaching and teaching. As Lazarus got worse, Mary and Martha decided they had better send for Jesus. When Jesus got the message, His disciples expected Him to drop everything and go to help Lazarus at once. They knew how much Jesus loved this man. The sisters also fully expected Him to come immediately. But Jesus did the strangest thing. He stayed just where He was for a few days. No one could understand this, as by now Lazarus was near death.

In John 11:4 Jesus says, "This sickness will not end in death. No, it is for God's glory so that God's Son may be glorified through it." In other words, this whole situation wasn't about Lazarus getting sick; there was a bigger picture being painted. When Mary and Martha's brother died, everyone was confused—except Jesus. He is never confused. He always knows what He is doing. He knew exactly what His dear friends and disciples would learn. They would learn something new about Him!

When Jesus eventually arrived at Bethany, Lazarus had been dead four days. The sisters asked the Lord the question that everybody must have been thinking: *Why didn't you come?* "If you had been here," Martha and Mary protested, "my brother would not have died" (John 11:21, 32). Undoubtedly this was the truth. They all knew Jesus could heal. But Jesus wanted to teach them something that would expand their souls and grow their faith. He wanted to teach them that He was not just a great healer but the Resurrection and the Life. So He raised a man to life who had been dead four days, and He did it in front of witnesses. What great glory was brought to God!

Through this experience, those close to Jesus learned a greater lesson, and sometimes that can be reason enough for the seemingly unfathomable behavior of a God who appears to be paying no attention whatsoever to our urgent demands. It is certain that after this event Lazarus was able to say like Job, "Though he slay me, yet will I trust him!" (13:15).

I remember being in the hospital, clutching my stomach and wondering why the medicine the doctors had prescribed just wasn't working. The situation provoked me to pray. Not that I was in the habit of invoking the Almighty, but I was a coward and wanted Him to save me from having surgery. If the medication had been effective, I would have been more convinced than ever that God has the power to heal bodies. God, however, wanted me to trust Him, to teach me "the greater thing." He wanted to show me how He was much more concerned with our souls than our bodies!

My appendix was duly removed, but complications led to my being retained for another operation. The situation gave me a chance to get to know my ward mates. In this hospital patients' beds lined the walls of large rooms; probably thirty of us in all shared a common healing station. The Sunday after my second operation, one of the nurses told me she wished she could go to church, but duty called. Without thinking, I offered a suggestion. "Why don't you help me into a wheelchair, and I'll lead a service right here for all of us. Church can come to you!" I was nineteen years of age, had never led a service in my life and was only a few months old in Christ. I couldn't believe I had asked her for such a liberty and was flabbergasted when she said, "That's a great idea!" She immediately announced to everyone in the ward that the church service would begin in one hour, and before I could protest, she said, "I'll tell the other people in the wards on this floor too, as there will be patients there who'll want to come. By the way," she added as an afterthought, "what religion are you?" "I don't know," I answered honestly enough. "I've only just got myself converted!" This didn't seem to dampen the nurse's enthusiasm one little bit, and she disappeared like the town crier rousing a sleeping neighborhood!

I panicked. Why on earth had I offered to do such a thing? What would I say? Turning to God, I prayed fervently that He would give me some ideas.

An hour later, true to her word, the head nurse wheeled in the blind, halt and maimed! Others walked into my ward all by themselves and sat in the visitors' chairs beside the patients' beds. Sitting in my wheelchair, I suggested we all sing some favorite hymns, which we did. I saw a few people nearby give me an odd look as if to say, "I hope she talks better than she sings," but I ignored them and made "a joyful noise to the Lord" (I was so glad the Bible said "joyful" and not "tuneful"). Then it was my turn, and I did the best I could. At the end of my talk, patients wanted to ask me questions, and I found myself whizzing round the ward in my wheelchair at a tremendous lick, doing my best to answer them.

Suddenly, I learned *the greater thing*: God was saving souls. This was a far greater thing than saving me from a second surgery! And God was telling me that He was trustworthy. He gave me something to say about Him that got people's attention and even helped me to introduce one girl to Christ! Yes, trusting

God to teach me something new about Himself became the object of my growing faith from that time on.

Above all, the thing God wants us to learn about Him is that He has our greater good in mind. He works in the circumstances He allows for our greater good and in order that we may see Him more clearly. Job said, "I had heard about you before, but now I have seen you" (42:5, TLB). Suffering is a magnifying glass, and like all magnifying glasses, it works both ways. When you look at God through the glass panel of pain, He appears bigger than you have noticed before. If you look at yourself through the other side of the glass, you appear smaller and more inadequate. One thing I have observed is that because pain drives me to refocus on God's "size"—His might, power and ability—I am more ready to cast my care in His direction, more ready to trust that He knows what He is doing, whatever happens to me. Job said, "God may kill me for saying this—in fact, I expect him to. Nevertheless, I am going to argue my case with him" (Job 13:15, TLB). Determining to fathom "the greater good" can provide us with even more energy for facing life's struggles.

No book on the subject of pain can be written without Joni Eareckson Tada coming to mind. At age seventeen Joni dove into a lake and broke her neck, causing paralysis from the neck down. Her story is movingly told in books and on film. Joni draws our attention to the importance of the spiritual over the physical. After agonizing adjustments Joni says, "My paralysis has drawn me close to God, and given a spiritual healing which I wouldn't trade for a hundred active years on my feet."[1]

Joni testifies to God's mercy, love and compassion. She writes, paints and sings of the grace of God in her life. Her whole life has been a magnifying glass, expanding our perception of God.

If I were to give an acrostic of grace, it would be:

God's
Reality,
Arming
Christians'
Experience!

Years ago, Joni accepted an invitation to speak in Milwaukee. I had the privilege of accompanying her to the auditorium. We waited, along with many businesspeople, to get into the hotel elevator. Joni was radiant. I could see the surreptitious glances the other people were giving her. No one in the elevator was talking. So I asked Joni what she was going to talk about at the auditorium, and when she said "Grace—and I'm going to sing about it too," there were more glances, and a few interested faces turned toward her. Then she began to practice!

I wish I could have captured the reactions on film. She still had a verse to go when we exited the elevator on the ground floor. There were many tears on the faces of the people. Joni sang "songs in the night" (Ps. 77:6), pointing people to a God of gracious enabling. Her trust shamed those of us who could walk out of that elevator on our own two legs. She would say that God has her greater good in mind. Her God is her heavenly Father who has promised never to leave her nor forsake her.

When our children were small, David, our six-year-old, hurt his arm. I called the doctor, and after a visit he made an appointment for an X-ray. David had the accident on Friday, and the doctor assured me it would be fine to wait until Monday to go to the hospital. My husband told David he could stay home from school because he was going for an X-ray.

The weekend over, and the time having arrived for the appointment, Stuart told David it was time to go. Our son seemed to be very reluctant to get into the car. On the way to the clinic, my husband glanced at him and saw that he was white and trembling. "Dave," he said, as reassuringly as he could, "there's nothing to be frightened about. It's only an X-ray, and I'll stay with you all the time."

"Don't tell me there's nothing to be frightened about, Dad," our little boy replied. "I know what an execution is!"

My husband and I were aghast that the poor child had had to wait three days with this on his mind! The amazing thing was that he turned up! But then, Dave has always been somewhat sanguine. He got into that car saying, in effect, "Though he slay me, yet will I trust him." It was his father who had made the arrangements. Somehow, it had to be all right, and his dad had promised not to leave him alone for one minute. Oh, that we could all have such trust in our heavenly Father.

Learning Something New about Myself

If trusting God during the trouble He allows to visit my life teaches me something new about Him, it also teaches me something new about myself. Learning trust (which I can never learn unless I have something to trust God for) shows me how far I have to go in my own growth and development. It shows me the caliber of my faith. Sometimes, in our daydreams, we run through some possible scenarios of suffering in our minds and imagine ourselves coping. I have often done this. First, you set the scene. Someone you love has just been killed in a car crash. The policemen knock at the door to bring the bad news. I see myself receive it with grace and ask them in, give them a cup of tea (the English always do that in times of crisis) and witness to them of life after death. Somehow we dream away and see ourselves doing a halfway decent job! But I have found that reality is another thing altogether.

When I was a child, the Second World War drove my father to move his family to England's Lake District. A particularly vicious air raid resulted in our piling into the car and running as far away from the bombs as we could. Seeing that everyone was doing the same thing, my father purchased a sturdy little cabin cruiser and deposited us on it until he could find suitable housing in our new environment. We two children loved living on the beautiful lake. We learned to be up early in the morning, dive over the side for a quick bath, and be ready for breakfast and school in no time flat.

I will never forget breaking the thin film of ice on the lake as winter came. It made us gasp and splutter, and mother would cook extra bacon and eggs, knowing what the experience would do to our appetites! No matter that we knew how cold that water was and no matter how equipped we believed we were to face it, no amount of mental preparation could help us with the actual experience of jumping into that cold water.

In the same way, no matter how well we think we have prepared ourselves for the troubles we know will be our lot, no matter how much we've rehearsed our part, the actual experience takes our breath away. It's like diving into that ice-cold water. You know exactly what ice-cold water must feel like. You are prepared to pay the price and plunge in anyway, believing that, once submerged, you are equipped to cope. As soon as you hit the water, however, the shock takes your breath away, and you find yourself gasping and spluttering. You are surprised at yourself, but you are learning something new.

Pain *really* hurts. Bodies *really* bleed. And trauma is traumatic! The mind can do its best to prepare us, but when we are in over our heads, we will find out exactly who we are and what our trust is made of.

What Does It Mean?

1. What is the difference between resignation and acceptance?

2. What have you learned about God through the tough things that have happened to you? What have you learned about others? About yourself?

3. Read the end of the story of Joseph and his brothers in Genesis 50:15–21. Discuss verse 20. What does this tell us about what Joseph believed about the troubles that came to him?

4. Read Philippians 1:12, where Paul voices sentiments similar to Joseph's. In verses 13–14 Paul explains two things that helped others because of the trouble that came to him. What are these two things? What is Paul able to do as a result (1:18)? Why is this example so hard to follow?

5. Look up these references and accumulate some information about trust.

    • Psalm 56:4

    • Psalm 119:42

    • Proverbs 3:5–6

    • Proverbs 11:28

    • Proverbs 28:26

    • John 14:1

6. Those who trust in the trustworthy One become like Him. According to First Corinthians 4:2 and Luke 16:10, in what ways should we be trustworthy?

7. Read the story of Daniel in the lions' den in Daniel 6. Trust develops as we develop holy habits. What habits did Daniel have (6:10)? Why isn't it safe to put your trust in people, even important and influential ones who like and admire you? What do you think Daniel prayed for while he was in the den? What would you have prayed for? Do we always get delivered from the lions' den? What should we trust God to do for us while we are there? What effect should our trusting God in our situation have on everybody around us?

How Should I Pray?

- Pray that God will help you to accept what you cannot change and use it as a springboard for action.

- Pray for those you know who are finding it hard to trust God in difficult circumstances.

- Pray about one aspect of trust you need to develop.

- Pray for those in authority.

- Pray for those believers like Daniel, serving or in contact with authorities who don't know God.

- Pray for those in the lions' den.

CHAPTER FIVE

WHEN FEELINGS FAIL YOU

If only I knew where to find him.

JOB 23:3

If I say, "Surely the darkness will hide me and the light become night around me," even the darkness will not be dark to you; the night will shine like the day, for darkness is as light to you.

PSALM 139:11–12

IT'S truly hard to cope with feelings that overwhelm us or, worse, to go through difficult times without any good or comforting feelings. When we deal with the unseen world—the world of faith and spiritual life—it's even harder. When it's so dark all around us that we can't "see" or "feel" God at all, we are tempted to put our trust in a real, live, concrete person and not in an unseen Spirit. And yet the growing we do at this level is really independent of feelings, sight and touch. It has to do largely with the unseen, not the seen; the unknowable, not the knowable; and with God, not us.

If there is one major lesson I have learned about myself in times of trouble, it is that I need to live in my "knowings" and not my "feelings," because I cannot trust my feelings. My feelings leave me gasping and spluttering as I dive into the cold waters of trouble. This is hard for those of us who like to live our lives in the feeling realm. And it's especially hard when we are hurting through our physical and emotional senses. Job struggled with this. He needed someone to touch him. He needed to feel his wife's arms around him. But the Scriptures say she wouldn't come near enough to comfort him with that loving touch he so desperately needed. "My breath is offensive to my wife," he said. We get a sense of Job's feelings about his feelings in chapter 23. Job wanted, above all else, to "connect" with God, to sense His real and necessary presence. But he couldn't "find Him." It was as if God did not exist in Job's personal universe anymore. "If only I knew where to find him," he laments. "If only I could go to his dwelling! . . . But if I go to the east, he is not there; if I go to the west, I do not find him" (Job 23:3, 8). "Where is He?" Job cries out. He cannot see God's face. He feels that God is hiding from him. Above all, Job longs to talk to God about it all, but God seems to be absent. And Job is feeling this for perhaps the very first time in his life.

FEEL GOD WITH YOUR FAITH

A friend of mine has just died of cancer. Shortly after she was diagnosed, I spent a day with her. She was such a wonderful lady. She was emotional and relational in personality. She kept saying, "Jill, I can't feel Him near me anymore. All my life I've been able to feel Him near me, but now, just when I need Him the most, He's not there!" At this point my friend found out that, like Job, she had a clear choice. As Warren Wiersbe says, she "could 'curse God and die' or 'trust God and grow'!" Grow how? Grow in the area of her faith. She was to learn that when she couldn't feel God with her feelings, she could feel Him with her faith—and that felt different! The "feelings" of faith are feelings of knowledge—or "knowingness." The Holy Spirit, after all, doesn't come into our lives to do His deepest work in the shallowest part of us—our emotions. But rather He comes into our lives to do His deepest work in the deepest part of us—our knowings.

And that's the test that suffering brings. God doesn't test our feelings for Him but rather our faith in Him. He tests our trust!

At the end of Psalm 139, David prays, "Search me, O God, and know my heart; test me and know my anxious thoughts. See if there is any offensive way in me, and lead me in the way everlasting" (139:23–24). He knows that God knows everything about him. After all, God has created him—knitting him intricately together in his mother's womb. He believes that God sees his thoughts even before he, David, gets around to thinking them! So he opens up his life before God, acknowledging that God knows everything, and asks God to show him if there is any "offensive way" in him. "You can see my anxious thoughts, O God," he says. "Do these offend You?" Why would our anxious thoughts offend God? Perhaps because God expects us to trust Him with our anxieties.

God doesn't worry—but if He did, He would possibly worry about our worrying! He wants us to stop being anxious. He has promised to supply our needs. When our feelings grow anxious, our faith can calm our fears. We have a decision to make. God wanted Job to say, "I know You are there—even though, at this time, my feelings deny Your very existence. I feel so desolate." Our feelings about God can get in the way of our knowledge of Him. We can begin to believe He isn't there at all, simply because we can't sense His presence.

Yet, if by faith we can affirm what we know deep down in our souls, this will calm many of our frantic fears and bring the tranquility of order to our confusion.

The "Mind" of Our Spirit

"But," you may ask, "what happens when our mind goes as we get old?" Although the mind is our physical part that computes information and relays it to our spirits, "knowing" God is not, in the end, a thing of the physical mind. Understanding this has been a comfort to me.

For years I've been concerned about getting old and losing my mind! I'm sure you know the little rhyme that says:

My glasses come in handy,
My hearing aid is fine.
My false teeth are just dandy,
But I sure do miss my mind!

Seriously, though, I have known people of faith whose minds have disintegrated. If I know God in my "knowings" and the knowing part of me becomes confused, what will happen then? David McKenna, in his book *The Whisper of His Grace*, gives a personal illustration that has wonderfully released and relieved me. He has helped me realize that even though we may lose our sensibilities, our spirit goes right on knowing, even though perhaps we aren't aware of it. What a comfort that is! For the "knowings" I'm talking about are deeper than our physical mind, which will disintegrate.

My wife, Janet, and I have just returned from the funeral of her only brother who died unexpectedly at the age of sixty-seven. As I mentioned before, their ninety-two-year-old mother is in a nursing home [suffering from dementia]. When my wife told her about the death of her only son, nothing registered. We began to debate the wisdom of taking her to the funeral, but decided the family needed her presence even if she did not know what was going on. . . .

Entering a side door along a ramp for the handicapped, we were surprised to be ushered directly into the funeral parlor in full view of the mourners. Instantly, we saw on the faces of the family the value of her being there and we heard the audible gasp of surprise from our friends. For her, however, no sign of recognition let us know she was aware of being at her son's funeral despite the flowers, open casket, organ music and tears. Watching her closely I detected no light of awareness in her eyes as the officiating minister read the Scripture, gave the eulogy and offered a homily of comfort for the family.

But then, to close the service, the pastor asked us to join in the recitation of the Twenty-Third Psalm, which was printed on the order of service. At the sound of the first words, "The Lord is my shepherd . . ." a strong and firm voice began to lead the congregation. It was Mom. Without missing a single word, she led us through the Psalm. Awe swept over us as we realized that Mom's lifetime of reading, memorizing and quoting the Word of God brought her back to reality and became her promise when her only son died.

After dismissal, we took Mom forward to the casket. Squinting to see his face, she asked, "Is this my boy?" Janet answered, "Yes, it's Eldon." With full awareness now, Mom asked her next question, "Did he make it to heaven?" Again, Janet answered, "Yes, he's in heaven with Joyce and Daddy now."

With that word of assurance, Mom lapsed back into the fog of senility and rode home without another word. In her, we saw trusting love at work. As with Job, God's promise had been engraved on her heart and even after she had lost touch with reality, it came back to her in the evidence that God had answered her prayer and fulfilled His promise. Never again will I assume that spiritual communication stops when it appears as if the mind is gone. Despite the suffering of senility, a lifetime of love is holding Mom in communion with her Lord.[1]

"Though he slay me," said that particular mother, "yet will I hope in him!" Job was able to say, "I know [not "I feel"] that my Redeemer lives!" It is in the mysterious soul made by the Creator

God—to know Him in reality and to believe Him there—that faith operates.

And so we need to trust God with that soul trust, not our feelings. Suffering surely shows us how much we have been depending on our senses. Yet as someone has said, "The pursuit of God needs to be independent of the material comforts of the senses." A human being can live for God, fear God and trust God without receiving any reward of feelings to help him or her bear it all. If we can lay down our insistence upon "connecting" with God emotionally, then we will be able to say with Job, "But he knows the way that I take; when he has tested me, I will come forth as gold." We will be able to tell ourselves, "I know He knows," and we can take comfort in that. He is with us, though we see Him not, feel Him not or sense Him not. I believe that because He told me He is and He also assures me through Job's testimony that "he knows the way I take." God is not disinterested in or divorced from my dilemma.

CERTAIN OF GOD'S PRESENCE

Years ago I was chasing our two-and-a-half-year-old grandson around our daughter's house. I was the "child care" for the day, and I was finding it hard! "What do I do?" I inquired of my daughter as she left the house. "Just stay on him!" she replied with a grin, and then she was gone. It sounded easy enough, but by 11 a.m. I was done! Keeping up with that little dynamo was for athletes, not grandmas! I made myself a nice cup of tea and sat down. Lulled into complacency, I suddenly "heard" silence! Galvanized into action, I tore around the house calling his name. "Drew, where are you?" I found him almost immediately, about to do something he shouldn't. "Drew, don't—" I began. Drew stopped and looked at me with something akin to wonder in his eyes. "Youse evwewhere, Gwanma!" he murmured in awe.

"Right, Drew, omnipresent Gwanma!" I replied. Though Drew thought he had escaped me, he learned to his chagrin that he hadn't!

I thought of all the times that I believed myself to be alone—alone with my pain and suffering or my misdoing. I decided I would try to do a better job of looking up into my Father's face at times like that, and I promised myself that I would say, "Youse evwewhere, Father," in wonder, love and praise. Such faith grows us up. When trouble comes, we can either "curse God and die"—or trust God and grow!

The Bible talks so much of walking by faith and not by sight. The Word of God uses metaphors of light shining in the darkness of our minds. This is the light of knowledge that God is, that God is there, that God is good and that God is concerned with our well-being even when "being well" is not part of the big plan. God's face is really turned toward us, not away from us.

The story is told of a little boy who was fearful of going to bed. He was afraid of the dark. Instead of giving him a nightlight, his father decided to stay with him in the room, in the dark, until his son fell asleep.

"Are you there, Father?" asked the little boy, with a quiver in his voice.

"Yes, my son," replied the father.

"I can't see your face," said the son.

"But I am looking at you, and I am smiling," the father replied. Then the boy fell asleep. He couldn't see his father or feel his father's touch, but he heard his father's word, and he believed it and rested in the good of it.

THINKING THROUGH OUR MISERY

I don't know when Job lost the sense of God's presence, but I suspect it was when he was sick. At the end of chapter 2, we find him sitting in dust and ashes, covered from head to toe in boils, scraping himself with a piece of pottery. At the start of chapter 3, we find him cursing the day he was born. He does not curse God, his wife or his friends. He does not curse the Sabeans and Chaldeans, who stole his animals and killed his servants (Job 1:14–17). But he does curse the day he was born.

He is absolutely miserable. The pain and itching is indescribable. There is nothing quite so painful as an itch that won't quit. There is no clean, white hospital bed for Job. No nurse, no medicine, no sleep—no relief. His friends wisely do not ask him how he feels! They could see even while they were a considerable way off that he was near death. In fact, they sat with him for seven days—the period of mourning for the dead. Job describes his disease in graphic fashion at different times throughout this book. He says he is nothing but skin and bones (19:20), that his skin is decayed and blackened. He is not a pretty sight. It is hard to look at him, to smell him, to watch the ravages of the disease take their course. Yes, his friends are kind and wise in not asking, "How do you feel?" After all, how do you expect him to feel?

It is a far more helpful thing to inquire, "What do you think about all this?" One reason for this is that the sufferer may be able to pour out his thoughts and feelings in words that help him, and the comforter can also act as a sounding board for his pain. Job, however, is careful to direct his tirade against life lived in a fallen environment. He does not direct his anger toward God—or people. This, to my mind, has one clear advantage; if you don't feel bad about God, you are in a great position to receive His help.

Stuart and I have three children and, at this point, thirteen grandchildren. Three of those grandchildren were born within twenty-four hours of each other. Their names are David, Christina and Drew, but when they were little, we lovingly and wryly called them Search, Destroy and Demolition!

I was giving my daughter and son-in-law a rest for a few days and read my grandson his favorite story before putting him to bed. The book is called *Alexander and the Terrible, Horrible, No Good, Very Bad Day*, by Judith Viorst. Everything happens to Alexander, and he wonders why. "That's just how life is," his mother tells him. I finished the book, tucked Drew into bed alongside his eighteen-month-old brother, who was sleeping soundly, and went to bed.

In the middle of the night, I felt a little hand tapping my arm. Awake instantly, I switched on the light, and there was Drew. I looked at him in horror. He was covered from head to toe with chicken pox. I don't know whether it was the fact that he was scraping himself with a comb that made the words come to mind, but I exclaimed, "Oh, my little Job!"

"No, Nanna—it's Drew," he said earnestly, a little tear running down his cheek. "I'm having a terrible, horrible, no good, very bad day," he offered next. "Why should so many spots happen to I?" (He was getting his me's and I's sorted out!)

Poor little Drew. I didn't ask him how he felt—it was obvious that he felt dreadful. But we talked about the spots and getting sick and why we get sick. His hurt and distress were directed away from Jesus, who let the spots come, to the sad fact that, as Alexander's mother said, "some days are like that!"

Holding his little, bumpy body in a big, clean bath towel after a soothing oatmeal bath (my mother's remedy), I rocked him all night long. I told him I was sorry he felt so awful and that I would stay with him and try to make it go away as quickly as I could. "Will Jordan get it?" he asked me.

"Yes," I answered with sad certainty. Drew smiled, and I understood. Somehow there is some comfort in knowing that suffering is a universal experience. Suffering gives you an opportunity to learn something new about God and yourself. But it also reveals some things to us about other people. As we will see when we look at the responses of Job's friends, suffering brings out the best and worst in those around us, as well as in ourselves, and draws us to realize that Jesus is the safest place to turn. He alone can be trusted in our trouble.

What Does It Mean?

1. Fill in the acrostic with your most common and familiar feelings when trouble comes.

   Fear

   E

   E

   L

   I

   N

   G

   S

2. Fill in the acrostic with things that help you to trust God when feelings fail you.

   T

   R

   U

   S

   T

3. Relate an experience in which feelings failed you but God didn't.

4. Read Psalm 139. What does it tell us about

   - God's knowledge of us?

   - God's feelings for us?

   - David's knowledge of God?

   - David's feelings for God?

   Which is most important, knowledge or feelings, and why?

5. Read Matthew 26:36–45 and Luke 22:46. Jesus' feelings were failing Him. Which verses tell us this, and which words specifically describe it? What were the disciples feeling, and why?

6. It was what Jesus knew about Himself and His mission that helped Him when He was feeling low. Read John 17. What does Jesus know

   - about Himself?

   - about His Father?

   - about His disciples?

7. What emotions would Jesus' knowledge and faith have had to override? As you look through the words of His prayer, what emotions do you think He was experiencing?

How Should I Pray?

- Praise God for His total knowledge of you.

- Thank God that He didn't let His feelings hinder Him from loving us.

- Pray for your own faith to be strengthened.

CHAPTER SIX

WAITING IT OUT

You . . . have seen what the Lord finally brought about.

JAMES 5:11

We know that suffering produces perseverance; perseverance, character; and character, hope. And hope does not disappoint us, because God has poured out his love into our hearts by the Holy Spirit, whom he has given us.

ROMANS 5:3–5

JOB, as someone has put it, was in God's waiting room. He was finding it a very difficult place to be. It's all very well to accept the inevitable adversity that comes to those of us who live in this time bubble called "life after the Fall," and it's all right to realize that trusting during trouble helps us to grow up in our faith and to lean less upon our feelings. But just how long are we expected to go on doing all this accepting and trusting?

There is nothing quite as difficult as waiting. When we are in the middle of some particularly difficult situation, time appears to stand still. Our problem is exacerbated by our Western lifestyle and mind-set, which often reflect our "instant" society. In America it seems we cannot bear to wait for anything. What is more, we regard instant service and gratification almost as rights.

ON THE WAY TO SOON

Not long ago I found myself in such a place. As I hunkered down to wait my situation out, I couldn't help searching the

Scriptures for glimpses of hope that it would all soon be over. I realized I was on a journey—the journey to "soon." I couldn't help but notice how often that little word soon kept popping up in my Bible readings, and I remember complaining petulantly to the Lord, "Not 'soon'—'now.'" I didn't like being on the way to "soon" one little bit!

On one occasion I remember trying to comfort our two-and-a-half-year-old twin grandchildren, who were howling because their daddy had kissed them goodbye and was on his way to work. "He'll be back soon!" I shouted soothingly. It's hard to shout—soothingly—above twins' screams, but I did my best. My best effort, however, did not alleviate the pain of parting, and I realized at once how stupid my attempt had been. What, after all, does "soon" mean to a two-and-a-half-year-old? When one is a toddler who loves Daddy very much, comfort is when "soon" turns to "now"!

Listening to the amplified cries of children in distress, I have discovered it's the same for me. Like my grandchildren, I have real trouble with "soon." Waiting is not my favorite thing to do, especially when I've waited for something extremely important—a child to be conceived, a teenager to give just one little hint that he likes belonging to me, a relative to come to Christ. But nobody knows how quickly "soon" will be except God, and He doesn't tell! His knowledge is withheld not to tease us but to test us! Waiting for closure always exposes the caliber of my faith, the intensity of my patience and trust, and the shape of my character. But when I'm waiting for some particular, painful trial to be over, there's bound to be some bright, well-meaning saint who lovingly, and often with ill-concealed satisfaction, comes around to tell me how much deeper I'll be when it is finished. I want to scream, "I don't want to be deeper! I want to stay shallow and have the hurt go away!" Perhaps you are on that journey today.

Job had said, "When he has tested me, I will come forth as gold." Job knew he was in God's waiting room. That's what that little word "when" means; it points to sometime in the future. "When" is not now. Yet on this journey to "soon," we find something is happening to us. We are being "golded." There's nothing like the fires of affliction to put a gold glow on our souls—on our character.

Warren Wiersbe says, "God never wastes suffering. Trials work for us, not against us. . . . God permits trials that He might build character into our lives."[1] Paul puts it very well in Romans 5:3–5: "We know that suffering produces perseverance; perseverance, character; and character, hope. And hope does not disappoint us, because God has poured out his love into our hearts by the Holy Spirit, whom he has given us." Knowing that God is intent on painting us with gold sort of helps a little when you are "on the way to soon."

So waiting produces perseverance—endurance that toughens us up. James gives us a comment on the life of Job. Writing to Christians in the fires of persecution, James reminds them that they are sharing in a great heritage. The prophets suffered for their faith, he points out: "We know how happy they are now because they stayed true to him then, even though they suffered greatly for it" (James 5:11, TLB). James then uses Job as a model of perseverance in the face of suffering. "You have heard of Job's perseverance," he says, "and have seen what the Lord *finally* brought about." Job's "soon" *finally* turned to "now," but by that time perseverance had produced a sterling spirituality. It seems to take time to "bring us forth as gold."

Improving Our Prayers

One thing that happens in God's waiting room is a marked improvement in both the quantity and quality of our prayers!

If anything can help to pull us in line with God's plan for our prayer life, it is time waiting in the waiting room.

Think about a hospital waiting room. All of us must have gone through the harrowing experience of waiting for our names to be called. It certainly helps soothe our apprehensions to have someone to talk to, doesn't it? In the same way, that part of our ongoing relationship with God we call prayer becomes the conducive environment for a talk with Him about our fears and phobias. It's sad, really, that suffering has to pay us a visit before we get around to paying God a visit and getting our prayer life back in shape, but that's the way it is with many of us.

One of the things I have learned as I'm waiting for it all to be over is to pray in the absence of rewards. As we grow in our relationship to God, we come to realize that prayer is a whole lot more than a heavenly shopping list; it is our lifeline to God. We learn to say, "Lord, what will You show me, teach me, or make of me?" rather than, "Lord, what will You give to me or do for me?" So often we feel self-righteous when we pray—as if God owes us something and will reward us as a master rewards his pet dog that begs in the right way for a biscuit. If we pray expecting to be rewarded with a "treat" (the answer to our prayer request), we have not advanced very far in the school of prayer. The problem of praying without rewards, however, is that we can become discouraged. We must exercise perseverance if for no other reason than Jesus' exhortation to pray—even when nothing seems to be happening at all (see Luke 18:1–8).

I will never forget being in God's waiting room on one occasion and praying on and on for something important to happen. I expected to see some sign of "God activity" in this serious situation, but I could see nothing to encourage me. Sitting by a still lake early one morning, I asked the Lord why my prayer effort was not being rewarded.

What reward do you want? I seemed to hear Him asking me.

"Well, Lord," I said, "it's not as if I'm asking You to wave a magic wand and make this situation disappear—I'd be quite content just to see some small evidence that You are involved in this. Some little sign that You are working some good out of all this trouble."

As I sat looking at the pretty lake, God put this startling thought into my mind: *Jill, do you believe there are fish in this lake?*

"Yes, of course."

Then God's still, small voice asked me another question: *How do you know? You see no evidence. The surface of the water is like glass!* Then, *Jill do you have to see a fish jump to believe that they are there?*

I knew well enough what the Lord was asking me: *Jill, do you have to see a sign to believe I am hearing and answering your prayers? Know only the fish are there. I always hear and always answer. Trust the timing to Me!* I tried from then on not to schedule His answers on my timetable and to trust God to work out His plan—how, where and when He would.

Living in Hope—Without Answers

When you're waiting on the Lord and not the answers, you've saved yourself a lot of stress. Job, stretched to the limits of his faith to remain true to God, was able to accept suffering that was a mystery to him, in part because he knew it was not a mystery to God. At this point he didn't demand answers from a deity who had not seen fit to give any. He sought, instead, a framework of hope to live in. "This vision does not reveal the why of the particular sufferings of Job or any other believer, but it does present the servants of God with a framework for hope."[2]

To live in hope without answers goes against our American grain, doesn't it? We are in danger of believing we have an inalienable right to know all we want to know! We ask ourselves, *How can we have hope if God doesn't explain the whole thing to us?* Yet Job finds hope when the answers don't come, and he learns to endure, to persevere while he is waiting.

There is some suffering, and Job's falls within this category, that deals with the type of darkness most of us would call irrational evil—suffering that doesn't make any sense at all. It is the disproportionate amount of suffering inflicted upon one person that disorients, confuses and often threatens to destroy our understanding of God. Yet the book of Job insists that all suffering falls within the sweep of God's sovereignty and is part of this life's experience. As we respond as He would have us respond—as we persevere in it—we find that our character is molded after Christ.

It's hard to get excited about growing character though, isn't it? I don't know about you, but when trouble arrives on my doorstep, the development of my Christian character is not very high on my agenda. It's beyond my tiny reach, when I'm reeling from the shock of a black day, to utter—as Job did—some of the brightest words of history! Yet as Warren Wiersbe says in *The Bible Exposition Commentary*, "God can grow a mushroom overnight, but it takes many years and many storms to build a mighty oak!"[3] His comment raises this question: *do we want to be mushy mushrooms or mighty oaks?*

During our children's teenage years, we had a beautiful old oak tree in our front yard. As my husband and I raised our three kids through the normal turbulence of adolescent challenges, there was many a time I would get out of the house and look at that mighty oak tree. After I had told myself, *You don't grow one of these overnight*, I would feel ready to go back into the house, face the kids and get on with the job at hand. As storms hit our area, I often watched that huge shadow bending and weaving and could almost see the way the roots would cling to the ground. I knew the tree had grown a little bit stronger from having survived the storm.

Paul reminds us in Romans 5:2–4 that we can "rejoice in the hope of the glory of God. Not only so, but we also rejoice in our sufferings, because we know that suffering produces perseverance; perseverance, character; and character, hope." As A.W. Tozer says, "Keep your feet on the ground but let your heart soar as high as it will. Refuse to be average or surrender to the chill of your spiritual environment."[4] Job refused to be average and did not surrender to the chill of his spiritual environment. The devil, of course, wants to paralyze us with the pain of waiting. God wants us to wait, to grow hope in our hearts, till everything is back to normal again.

SPIRITUAL GIANTS—OR FREAKS?

In the years we were raising our three children, I went through a hard waiting period. I was waiting for them to grow up! We had three perfectly normal kids, but I, like Job, became obsessed with fears of the future catastrophes that might occur. ("What I feared has come upon me; what I dreaded has happened to me.") *What would I ever do if our children didn't "make it" spiritually?* I asked myself daily. Every time we had an argument—even a little tussle over minor things—especially in their teenage years, I felt I shouldn't function as a Bible teacher, counselor or Christian writer until all was well between us again! How could I talk about Christian values if things were not in absolute harmony at home? I began to refuse invitations to speak. When all was "perfect" on the home front, I reasoned, I would have earned the right to get out on the spiritual battlefront to win the war! All the devil had to do to effectively silence me was keep me off balance in one of my relationships.

It was about this time that a publisher asked Stuart and me to write a book about raising teenagers. "Never," I responded emphatically, when my husband read me the letter.

"Why not?" he asked.

"Because we don't have perfect kids yet," I replied quickly.

"Very true," was his rejoinder, "but if you're going to wait till they are spiritual giants, the book may never get written!"

"What do you mean?" I asked, shocked into listening.

"Well, Jill, you seem to be waiting for the children to become spiritual giants before you'll minister in this particular way. Giants are freaks! I don't want to raise spiritual freaks. Our kids are not perfect, but they are perfectly normal Christian kids, and we are perfectly normal Christian parents. Let's write about that."

And so we did. I learned to tell Satan to get lost and got on with my responsibilities. I worked on all my close relationships, as much as it depended on me; then I left the rest to the Lord, waiting on Him for my orders and not allowing other people's behavior to control my actions.

A STRATEGY FOR WAITING

How did Job deal with this waiting period in his life—this period of great loss and sickness before God brought any resolution? We see some indications that he was doing his best to go on with life. And we know that, in the eyes of heaven, Job was seen to have "persevered," according to James, who wrote about it centuries later. Still, some of the blanks aren't filled in for us. But there are other "Jobs" in Scripture who have something to say to us about waiting. Our own life experiences and those of Jobs we have known can give us guidance during the dark periods that seem never-ending.

Keep Up Your Routines

Satan would paralyze us with the pain of waiting and whisper in our ears, "Wait until things are back to normal before you get back into your routine." But life doesn't work that way. We still have the intact parts of our lives demanding our attention. Maybe we've lost a spouse, but we have the children to tend to. Maybe we've lost a job, but there's plenty to do at home as we job-hunt. And no matter what we've lost, there is the day-to-day upkeep of our bodies and our homes.

I know that hobbies help me at such times. Choosing to do something that has been an important part of my life and schedule—something that I enjoy doing—can relieve stress and begin the healing process.

Plants, for instance. During particular periods of stress in my life, I've found myself attacking the job with added ferocity. I repot, prune, water and manure with frantic energy. A friend dropped by to see me on one such day and asked, "Where is that neat tree that stood by the door?" I pointed to the bush that sat meekly in the same place! "Stressed?" my friend inquired sympathetically, gazing at what was left of the tree. "Stressed," I replied. "I'll pray for you," she promised. Routine helps to reestablish normal patterns of life for us and makes us feel a little bit more secure.

After Jesus was crucified and resurrected, there was a waiting period for his disciples. He had appeared to them a few times, but the Holy Spirit had not come yet. In John 21 we can almost hear Peter's restlessness when he announces, "I'm going fishing." Of course! That's what he had done all his life until he became a follower of Jesus. As it turned out, the risen Jesus came to meet him and the other disciples on the seashore, calling out to them as they came in after fishing all night without success. First, He told them where to throw their nets, and then, when they had brought in a miraculous haul of fish, He invited them to share the breakfast

He was cooking! It was a time for routine. Later, when the Holy Spirit came, their lives would take a new turn; it was, in fact, at the conclusion of this seashore breakfast that Jesus spoke with Peter quite frankly about the changes that would come to his life. But for now, in the midst of their unanswered questions and the pain of being without their Teacher, doing the familiar thing helped.

Keep Up Your Relationships

We hear Job lamenting his loss of relationships in 19:13–19:

He has alienated my brothers from me;
my acquaintances are completely estranged from me.
My kinsmen have gone away;
   my friends have forgotten me.
My guests and my maidservants count me a stranger;
   they look upon me as an alien.
I summon my servant, but he does not answer,
   though I beg him with my own mouth.
My breath is offensive to my wife;
   I am loathsome to my own brothers.
Even the little boys scorn me;
   when I appear, they ridicule me.
All my intimate friends detest me;
   those I love have turned against me.

Sometimes people cannot cope with other people's pain because they don't want to confront their own mortality. At other times they feel helpless or don't know what to say, so they just keep out of the way. Maybe some of Job's friends believed his disease was contagious and didn't want to get sick. Maybe some among them believed his suffering was well deserved—and who were they to interfere with God's dealing with a sinner? For whatever reason, when suffering came to Job, alienation came along with it.

We can tell that Job was trying to keep relationships going simply because he lists others' disappointing responses to him.

See how many people were affected—brothers, acquaintances, guests, maidservants, wife and intimate friends. Even "those I love have turned against me." These words sound so similar to what the apostle Paul stated in Second Timothy 1:15: "You know that everyone in the province of Asia has deserted me." Considering all the persecution Paul encountered during his ministry, it is not surprising to hear him say, "If it is possible, as far as it depends on you, live at peace with everyone" (Rom. 12:18). Paul had come to recognize that we are only responsible for our own attitude, not the attitudes of others. How often do we try our hardest to reach an understanding with someone or try to mend a relationship that seems intent on falling apart, only to realize that it will take more than our efforts to make it work? Most of us have a very real sense of the kind of bitterness Job encountered when those he loved turned away from him.

We must remind ourselves that Job managed to maintain an uneasy link with four of his friends right to the end of his trials, and in chapter 42 we see him thoroughly reconciled with everyone.

> All his brothers and sisters and everyone who had known him before came and ate with him in his house. They comforted and consoled him over all the trouble the LORD had brought upon him, and each one gave him a piece of silver and a gold ring. (42:11)

I don't know if that happy outcome would have occurred if Job had not struggled to keep the door of reconciliation open. How differently it might have turned out if he had simply "written off" the people in his life. Are we able to wait out these difficult seasons in our relationships? Or when we get no response, do we throw up our hands in frustration and say, "This takes too much energy. If that's how they want it, that's the way they can have it"?

I have a good friend whose college-age daughter began to live with her boyfriend on campus. This caused considerable pain to her parents, who, in all good conscience, could not condone this behavior. Their relationship with their daughter became extremely tenuous. Then they began to make serious efforts to use the situation as a bridge instead of allowing it to become a barrier. They invited the young man home for the holidays. (The daughter had not been coming home because of the situation.) They accepted him into the family—although separate bedrooms were insisted upon while their daughter's boyfriend was in their house—and eventually won him to Christ. This did not sit well with their daughter, and the situation is not yet resolved, but a fragile link was established with a hopeful resolution in sight. I admire my friends' Job-like courage and perseverance, and I believe God will bring His blessings to their family in His time.

Keep the Faith

It isn't easy to continue going to church or trying to exercise a ministry during, or immediately after, a period of pain and suffering—and yet there is healing if we do so. I know how difficult it can be to go to a worship service and hear everyone singing happy hymns. *One more happy chorus and I'll scream!* you think. But there is a certain therapy in worship and service. This is true because in ministry we often meet a lot of people a whole lot worse off than we are. It's like the old saying, "I was sad because I had no shoes—until I met a man who had no feet!" In Christian service we usually bump into quite a few people who have no feet! In helping and encouraging them, we find a measure of relief ourselves.

What did Jesus' followers do while they were waiting for the Comforter to come after Jesus had ascended into heaven? "They all joined together constantly in prayer" (Acts 1:14). They also went to a great deal of trouble to choose a disciple to take the place of Judas, who had killed himself after betraying Jesus—and can't you imagine the emotions this process brought up for all of them? At this point their only instructions were to wait for the Holy Spirit. They waited in faith, restoring the apostles' number back to the original twelve in the anticipation that their little organization—their body of Christ—would indeed move forward and continue Jesus' ministry on earth. On the day of Pentecost, "they were all together in one place" (2:1). During their wait, all they knew to do was pray and stay together—and that's what they did.

I find the examples of these faithful people practical and helpful. While I am in God's waiting room, I can realize that my character is under divine reconstruction. I can try to normalize my routine (with lots of English cups of tea and a big pair of pruning shears or similar helps). I can continue my religious disciplines, whether I am feeling "connected" or not, and keep up whatever ministry is feasible for me. I can also try to mend whatever fences I can and try not to worry too much about the ones that only God can mend at some future date. Persisting in all of this will help me regain my spiritual perspective.

Are you in God's waiting room? Are you waiting for a baby to be born? A prodigal to return? A spouse to reconcile? Are you waiting for someone to share your life with? For a job? For a cure? Wait on the Lord and not on the answer. Try to concentrate on His person, His plans and schedule—His business. Job's growing faith did not stop the agony, but it helped him find a measure of productivity in his life, to the extent that the Scriptures say, "As you know, we consider blessed those who have persevered. You have heard of Job's perseverance and have seen what the Lord finally brought about."

What Does It Mean?

1. Share with a group (two minutes) or write a paragraph about your hardest "waiting room" experience.

2. Read James 5:7 and discuss or record your answers to these questions:

    • Why do you think James uses the figure of the farmer to illustrate patience?

    • What is the incentive to have patience and why?

    • James says we consider "blessed" those who persevered (5:11). In other words, these sorts of people were seen as heroes. Do you think this is still true today? Explain.

3. Read Philippians 4:6–7. The different words for prayer in this passage are *prayer*, *petition*, and *thanksgiving*. How are these terms different from each other?

    • Which one is hardest to engage in when you are in trouble?

    • Which type of prayer, if any, do you think is most important?

4. Discuss or write about the following quotes. Which speaks to you, and why?

    • *Warren Wiersbe:* "Do you want to be mushy mushrooms or mighty oaks?"

    • *A. W. Tozer:* "Refuse to be average or surrender to the chill of your spiritual environment."

5. Share or meditate on one practical thing you do that relieves stress when you are in God's waiting room.

6. Read Isaiah 40:28–31. What does it mean to hope in the Lord? Why do you think Isaiah uses the figure of a young man (40:30)? What, for you, is most difficult about waiting?

7. Worry can distract us from trusting. We worry, like Job, that bad things lie ahead for us or for our children. Take five to ten minutes to put Matthew 6:25–34 into your own words. Use as few "Bible words" as possible.

8. Another translation of the word *wait* is "hope." It means "to look expectantly; to have confidence in." Read the following verses. Discuss their meanings, or reflect on them in writing.

    • Psalm 37:7–9

    • Psalm 40:1

    • Isaiah 26:8

    • Isaiah 30:18

    • Isaiah 51:5

9. Read Luke 18:1–8 and spend some time discussing it or writing about it. What is the lesson, as stated in verse 1?

How Should I Pray?

• Pray that you will be disciplined in the devotional habits that will create an environment for waiting on Him.

• Pray for your church leaders and missionaries—that they will always pray and not give up.

• We can be waiting on the Lord or waiting on disaster. The difference is whether or not we are trusting in God. Trust is developed through prayer. Pray through Matthew 6:25–34 for yourself, paraphrasing the verse. Pray through it again for others.

ʃHOW TO COMFORT JOB

*No one said a word to him, because they saw
how great his suffering was.*

JOB 2:13

*Now the body is not made up of one part but of many. . . . If one part
suffers, every part suffers with it; if one part is honored, every part rejoices
with it. Now you are the body of Christ, and each one of you is a part of it.*

I CORINTHIANS 12:14, 26–27

HAVE you ever lost someone close to you? Perhaps they lived far away, yet you found yourself saying, "I have to go." So you packed a bag and traveled, maybe a considerable distance, just to be there with family and friends. And what happened when you arrived? You were greeted at the door, and you simply said, "I had to come." And somehow that was enough.

I am privileged to have served on the board of World Relief, a Christian agency. Their aim is to relieve suffering worldwide in the name of Christ. One summer they invited me to go to Croatia, just after the conflict with Serbia. This was during a period of uneasy peace. I joined a dozen other Christian women, and off we went. "What will we do when we get there?" we asked each other. We didn't know, but we met together at a specified place and traveled to Croatia to sympathize and comfort. The experience turned out to be life-changing.

That summer along the border of Serbia, we women met refugees—Croats, Serbs and Muslims—who, fresh from the horrors of war, told us their stories. We listened, took part in meetings, visited the camps and did various practical things. But mostly we kept saying, "We just had to come!" Over and over again they thanked us for "just being there." We learned that you have to get close enough to comfort—and that it will cost you. It will cost you time, possibly money, and it will most certainly involve some creative enterprise. It will also cost you emotional capital.

A MINISTRY OF PRESENCE

There were some people in Job's life who just "had to come." He had many friends, but Eliphaz, Zophar and Bildad were special. They were Job's peers, worshiping the same God he did. Job held them in high regard and for good reason. When they heard about all the trouble that had come to Job, they set out from considerable distances, agreeing to meet at a certain point and travel together as brothers to sympathize and comfort their fallen friend.

When they arrived and saw Job from a distance, they could hardly recognize him. They began to weep aloud and, as their custom was, tore their robes and sprinkled dust on their heads. Then they sat on the ground with him for seven days and seven nights. "No one said a word to him, because they saw how great his suffering was" (Job 2:11–13).

There is no question about it; it costs to comfort. Job's friends went out of their way to comfort him. They packed up and traveled a considerable distance in a day and age when there were no upgrades or private planes to help ease the miles. They were leaders in their own right and chiefs of their own tribes. They left their homes, their families and their responsibilities at no small cost to be real friends. If friendship is to matter, there is no shortcut.

In chapter 30, verse 22, we get a vivid description of how Job is feeling: "You snatch me up and drive me before the wind; you toss me about in the storm." Who hasn't felt tossed about, at the mercy of forces beyond our control? It helps at such times to have the comfort of companions in the midst of the tempest.

If we want to help a Job, we will need to pay the price. It will cost us to comfort, and yet we need to go where our troubled brothers or sisters are, to visit their ash heaps in person if possible. There is something incredibly comforting about someone "just being there." In times of overwhelming distress, it helps to pool the resources—the ideas of other comforters. I wonder which one of Job's friends came up with the idea of taking a "compassion trip" and actually traveling all the way to Job's home to see him. I can imagine them talking with each other and brainstorming about which course of action to take. When someone is in trouble, it's a good idea to call together other concerned folk and put some serious thought and planning into alleviating the distress. That is why a church home is so important. In belonging to a body of local believers who can pray and support the weak, we multiply our gifts of mercy; this is what the church is all about.

Not long ago, Jill, a young mother at our women's meeting, had an aneurysm that burst. She was rushed to the hospital and placed on life-support systems. There was an instant outpouring of love and sympathy from the church, and a prayer chain was set up among the women. A few close friends closed ranks, meeting together at an appointed place and time to share ideas and offer time, money and gifts as each was able. Though Jill was still in a deep coma in intensive care, hours had been given to moving her limbs and talking to her, though they were told the young mother was in a vegetative state.

Months later, those women were still sitting on that "ash heap" with their friend, having mourned as if for one dead, and yet having witnessed a miracle as incredible as the raising of Lazarus! A group of elders and pastors came together at the request of the young husband to anoint Jill with oil and pray over her according to James 5:14–15. Our pastor of women's ministries told me she remembers vividly struggling to believe that the prayers being prayed would be answered and wondering if what they were saying or doing would have any effect at all.

At a women's board meeting, just three months later, one of Jill's closest friends and caregivers gave us an incredible report. "Jill is talking, responding to visitors, though they say her motor skills will take months to come back," she said with tears. "Her long-term memory seems to have returned completely, though her short-term memory has not." Our board carefully noted the ongoing prayer requests and recommitted time to continue in prayer.

Laurie, our pastor, told us of her ambivalence at the prayer service when the crisis first occurred and then said, "Jill told me yesterday that she remembers absolutely everything about it. She knew the people who were there and heard the prayers that were prayed!" Creative care continues as we trust God for total recovery. Together, Job's daughter Jill and her friends are rejoicing in God's grace, healing and mercy. It cost Jill's friends hours and hours of precious time—but then, it always costs to comfort!

LET YOUR TEARS TALK

Once Job's friends had come close enough to comfort, they expressed their deep concern in the custom of their culture: "When they saw him from a distance, they began to weep aloud" (Job 2:12). They let their tears talk. No one said a word to him because they saw how great his grief was.

Can you cry? Sometimes I can and sometimes I can't. I have discovered, as I have traveled "my Father's world that broke my Father's heart," that my Father's heart lives within me in the person of the Holy Spirit. I have learned to ask Him to pray for the hurting who need help "with such feeling that it cannot be expressed in words" (Rom. 8:26, TLB). There is a groaning and a grieving that expresses itself in tears, that only the Holy Spirit can produce in us. These are not crocodile tears, but Christ's tears.

I have been on the receiving end of such empathy too. I remember becoming hard and embittered because I was lonely. My husband's work took him away from the family for months on end. I knew I needed to talk to someone, but to whom? My senior missionary's husband traveled too, even more than mine. She seemed to be doing just fine! How could I possibly share my pain with her? She was sure to open her Bible and point me to some sacrificial text of Scripture that would emphasize my lack of spirituality. This situation was not what I expected when we left the business world to join a mission. After a miserable few weeks on that particular ash heap of my dreams, I summoned my courage and went to talk to my "model" of sufficiency.

I remember entering her office and seeing her toiling over mounds of paperwork. She was stretched to the limit with the responsibilities she carried and was busy like nobody else I knew. I felt guilty bothering her. She glanced up and saw, in the words of Job, "how great my grief was." Immediately she put her pen down, turned her chair around and gave me her full attention. She knew from years of experience that listening is akin to loving. Her body language said to me, "You are center stage in my thinking—talk to me!" I burst out then with my complaint. I told her I was fed up with the "Daddy space" in my children's lives, that I had tried to follow her example and be the perfect little missionary wife, but it hadn't worked. "I know you'll find this difficult to understand," I blurted out, "because you've been able to be all the things you should be—and find joy in it, but I only find pain." I stopped then and looked at her. I couldn't believe my eyes. She was crying—really crying. "It's hard, isn't it?" she said simply, reaching for the tissues. But it wasn't those words that shouted out to me; it was her tears. The sound of tears talking cannot be escaped. "I can't believe I'm seeing what I'm seeing," I muttered. "You mean it's been hard for you too?" She laughed then, inviting me to sit down. Her sympathetic silence had encouraged me to tell her what was troubling me, but her tears told me it was all right to feel as I did. More than that, her tears told me that she felt the pain too. Her genuine concern assured me there was someone who had been there and survived, and that there could be victory and joy in the lonely times for me as well. It strikes me that all of us can probably do these two simple things for our friends. We can have a ministry of presence, and we can let our tears talk.

We are often so overwhelmed by the idea of seeing someone we love who is very ill—perhaps undergoing cancer treatment— or one who has been recently bereaved, that we tend to keep our distance. It's easier that way. Maybe we are willing to go but are intimidated by the thought of having to say something once we get there. *I'm not qualified enough, spiritual enough, experienced enough*, we tell ourselves. *Perhaps I'll say the wrong thing and make matters worse.* Yet Job's friends went and expressed their concern their way. We can at least attempt to do the same. Perhaps it would not be appropriate for us to tear our robes, cry aloud and sprinkle dust on our heads as they did, but we can put our arms around Job, his wife or his children and do it in the way most suited to our personalities and situations. We can find ways to "weep with those who weep" (Rom. 12:15, NKJV).

Significant Silence

The friends, at least, took the trouble to visit Job's ash heap and sit on it with him; that was not a comfortable thing to do for seven days. Remember, seven days was the period of mourning for the dead! They felt they were coming to his funeral before it happened. Once they had a good look at him, they had very little doubt that Job was not long for this world. So, "No one said a word to him, because they saw how great his suffering was" (Job 2:13). These friends were not afraid of silence.

We are so afraid of silence in our noisy culture. We believe we must fill silence with words, whether we have anything significant to say or not. And yet sometimes someone else's suffering is so intense that silence is the only appropriate response. Don't feel you have to say something. There is something all of us—young or old, clever or timid, spiritually deep or not so deep—can do. At the very least, we can go, we can cry, and we can listen lovingly. There's nothing too difficult about that, and the amazing thing is that that's exactly where the ministry of encouragement begins!

In for the Long Haul

Another impressive thing about Job's comforters was the fact that they were in it for the long haul. Maybe Job didn't appreciate that fact as time wore on, but at least they didn't bail out at the first opportunity. If we are going to be real comforters, we are going to have to settle in to see it through. We may not be in a position to be absent from our home or business, but we can take steps to assure Job that we'll be there till the end.

A young woman in our church lost her husband to cancer. For the first year of her loss, her friends, family and even strangers rallied around and ministered to her. Then came the second year—the year the experts say is usually the worst. "I hope they are right," she wrote to me, "because this second year has been the pits! It was great at first, with so many wonderful people giving me their full attention, but now they are busy with their own lives, and I'm all alone."

It's obviously not possible for everyone to keep up such intensive attention, but some should. I am learning to ask God, "Do you want me to be in this for the long haul?" Sometimes He says no, and sometimes He says yes. If He replies in the affirmative, it's extremely important to be faithful. And if we are the ones who should stick around until He says it's over, we should take steps to learn what to do and what to say. You can't stay silent forever, and you have to blow your nose and dry your eyes at some point, and then it will be time to talk. When that time comes, we had better be equal to the task. Otherwise we may earn the same rebuke Job's friends heard eventually because they had not "spoken rightly."

There can be great comfort in words. But that all depends on what the words are and when we use them. Our words should always have their basis in Scripture. These are the words that can be used by the Holy Spirit to comfort and heal. They certainly should not be words of rebuke or criticism. When Job's comforters later break their silence and become his critics, we see Job's suffering intensify. After all, relational pain can be the deepest and most intense pain of all. "Sticks and stones may break my bones, but words will never hurt me," the saying goes. I don't believe that, do you? Words can cut far deeper than a stone and beat one's feelings red-raw. Our words need to be carefully chosen and applied to heal and help, not to hurt, even if the suffering is a result of person's foolishness or bad choices.

Then the words need to be applied at the right time. I'm sure you have been the victim of "right" words spoken at the wrong time! Timing is vitally important when we are trying to encourage someone. Ecclesiastes 3:7 tells us that there is "a time to be silent and a time to speak."

I remember working with a young teenager. She had been promiscuous before she found the Lord and had very little home support once she became a believer. She struggled on but fell into her old ways again. One day she came to tell us she was pregnant and her parents wouldn't let her come home. I remember feeling pretty exasperated, looking at her standing on our doorstep. She knew better. She had seemed to really put things together, had gotten a job and had begun to turn her life around. How could she have been so foolish? And if she was going to have sex, why didn't she take precautions? Things needed saying, but not then. Now, in her extremity, she needed a bath, a meal, a hug and a bed! So I tried only to use wise words of welcome and told her I was so glad she had felt able to come to us in her trouble. That night, that was enough. There would be a time in the future when she would be ready to receive my words, but it wasn't now.

There is a difference between constructive and destructive criticism. Real love always looks for a way to be constructive. When Job's friends began to talk, they undid much of the good they had done. They began to accuse him and thereby did the devil's work for him.

What Does It Mean?

1. Read Job 2:11–13. Which of the following do you appreciate and why?

   • people who have comforted you at cost to themselves

   • a ministry of presence

   • tears that talk

   • companionship over the long haul

2. Share or write about an experience of trouble and how someone comforted you.

3. Read First Corinthians 12:20–26. What does this teach you about the body of Christ? about suffering with hurting "members"?

4. There are two sides to comfort: the comfort that is offered and the comfort that is received. Read Genesis 37:29–35.

Why wasn't Jacob comforted? Read First Samuel 1:5–18. Why couldn't Elkanah comfort Hannah? Why was she able to be comforted in verse 18? Read Psalm 23:4. Under what kind of circumstances can we find comfort? Read Psalm 77:2. Why might we refuse to be comforted?

5. Isaiah 40 begins with the words, "Comfort, comfort my people." When God gave this message to Isaiah, the people of Israel were in Babylonian captivity. Read Psalm 137, which was a response to their captivity. List the reasons people needed comforting.

6. Read Second Corinthians 1:3–7. The word *comfort* appears nine times. List the information you can gather from these five verses concerning how comfort works.

Optional for group time: Have one person share a "Job" situation (no names, two minutes). Then spend time getting input from the group about how true comfort might be given.

How Should I Pray?

- Pray for a particular situation you know about in which someone needs comfort.

- Pray for Christian counselors.

- Pray for the body of Christ and caregivers in your community.

- Pray for your own need for comfort in different areas of your life.

- Pray for those who need comfort but are refusing it for some reason.

- Pray for people who need to bear testimony to God's comfort in a difficult situation.

Chapter Eight

HOW TO HANDLE CRITICISM

I know that my Redeemer lives.

Job 19:25

*I care very little if I am judged by you or by any human court;
indeed, I do not even judge myself. My conscience is clear, but that
does not make me innocent. It is the Lord who judges me.*

I Corinthians 4:3–4

THE name Satan means "the accuser." This is how we are introduced to the devil in the book of Job. To accuse means "to blame, conjure, or charge." When we meet Satan in the court of God in Job 1, the Lord Almighty is busy commending Job. "Have you considered my servant Job?" He asks Satan. The accuser boldly starts to condemn the one whom God commends.

We see a similar, more ominous picture of Satan in Revelation 12:9–10. The apostle John describes for us his vision: "The great dragon was hurled down—that ancient serpent called the devil, or Satan, who leads the whole world astray. He was hurled to the earth, and his angels with him. Then," the apostle says, "I heard a loud voice in heaven say: 'Now have come the salvation and the power and the kingdom of our God, and the authority of his Christ. For the accuser of our brothers, who accuses them before our God day and night, has been hurled down.'" John sees Satan accusing the servants of the Lord "day and night." The devil is intensely hostile. He doesn't like us. He will never change his mind about what he thinks of us either, because he can never change who he has become, the personification of evil.

The apostle Paul depicts Satan as restlessly roaming around our world like a hungry lion, "looking for someone to devour" (1 Pet. 5:8). All his energies are bent on chewing us up and spitting us out, and he does this, or attempts to do it, in a variety of ways. One of his favorite tactics is to get us to do his accusatory work for him!

How would Satan get you or me to do his work? For an example, consider the time Jesus was setting off for Jerusalem, knowing it was extremely dangerous. It was time for him to die, but his disciple Peter would hear none of this death business. "You mustn't go!" he remonstrated. Whereupon Jesus said to him, "Get behind me, Satan! You are a stumbling block to me; you do not have in mind the things of God, but the things of men" (Matt. 16:23). By refuting Jesus' viewpoint, Peter was actually speaking for Satan. Jesus recognized the devil's voice—and resisted his suggestion.

As we go about our world, meeting Job and his children, we need to be wary of how we advise these people who are in distress. We need to think twice, or three or even four times, before we break our empathetic, safe silence.

In the story of Job, his friends miss God's perspective entirely. Although they begin well, their words take them into the devil's territory. Fortunately, Job discerns a spirit of error behind the arguments and advice of his wife and friends. He knows God well enough to recognize counterfeit teaching.

How important it is to "learn God"—to understand how He thinks and works and feels. Over and over again Job rejects his friends' words, refuting them with truth. Yet his friends' arguments sound so correct. They are mixed with enough truth that only the truly discerning can see that something has gone wrong with the theology.

My husband worked in a bank before he went into full-time Christian work. He was chief assistant to the chief inspector. The job of the inspection team was to find and catch the bank employees who were getting the bank's money mixed up with their own. His training included sitting for hours and hours in a dusty vault, counting thousands of bank notes, among which had been hidden a handful of counterfeit ones. The idea was that if you were so thoroughly cognizant of the real thing, the counterfeit would be easy to spot.

There is no greater argument to my mind for getting to know God than the anticipation of suffering! Learning to know Him in the good times prepares us for what will be said to us in the bad times! In fact, the more solid and grounded we can be before a storm arrives, the better we will fare spiritually. Jesus said in John 10:4 that His "sheep" know His voice and will listen to Him. If His voice becomes familiar to us, we will more readily detect the counterfeit when we hear it.

One of the problems with advice is that it often comes from "qualified" Christians who speak with great authority, and we feel intimidated by their expertise. Who are we, we think, to question our elders—someone more mature in the faith than we are? We have been taught by Scripture to respect our leaders and listen to what they tell us. Their language sounds so right, so spiritual, that it's hard to find anything wrong in what they say. Yet Satan can use the most spiritual of words to do the deepest damage. Job knew all about this problem. He faced it in the persons of Eliphaz, Zophar and Bildad.

When Others Judge What You Do

Most of the book of Job comes to us in the form of oratory—the conversation and debate between Job and his friends. Together they are trying to make sense of what has happened to Job. What often happens when humans try to make sense of life is that they rely on the little human knowledge they have. We have our human systems, often quite logical to us, into which we try to fit the things that happen to us. Sometimes things fit, but often these events are just a bit too large for our understanding. It is in such situations that we must rely on God, whose understanding is big enough, though ours is not. The advice offered by Job's three friends gives us good examples of the different human (and limited) ways in which we react to the Job-like situations in our lives.

Eliphaz, the authority figure, speaks first. Eliphaz is the oldest and possibly the most experienced of Job's friends. His opinion, in essence, is "God is a God of majesty and justice who punishes sinners and rewards the righteous." He claims to know what God is like and how He behaves. Eliphaz can be a formidable friend! Have you ever had a friend like that—the sort of a person who knows an awful lot of theology and lets you know he knows? That can be pretty intimidating. The problem with an Eliphaz—an authority figure—is that he talks as though he has a special "in" with the Almighty.

> Consider now: Who, being innocent, has ever perished?
>   Where were the upright ever destroyed?
> As I have observed, those who plow evil
>   and those who sow trouble reap it. . . .
> Can a mortal be more righteous than God?
>   Can a man be more pure than his Maker?
> If God places no trust in his servants,
>   if he charges his angels with error,
> how much more those who live in houses of clay,

whose foundations are in the dust,
who are crushed more readily than a moth!
(Job 4:7–8, 17–19)

When someone who has had a lot of Christian experience informs you that God has told them to tell you something and then tells you in "Scriptury" words, it's hard not to be impressed! Who am I, you may ask yourself, to call into question such testimony? Eliphaz maintains that everyone knows God blesses the righteous and punishes sinners. In fact, if God punishes sin by sending suffering, and Job is suffering to such a great degree, he must be a pretty big sinner!

Job points out that reality teaches differently. "Have you never questioned those who travel?" he asks. "Have you paid no regard to their accounts—that the evil man is spared from the day of calamity?" (21:29–30). So often it is the righteous in this life who have it hard and the unrighteous who seem to get off scot-free.

Years later, another very wise man, Solomon, came to the same conclusion: righteous men get what the wicked deserve, and wicked men get what the righteous deserve (Eccles. 8:14). As I once heard author Philip Yancey say, "We must not confuse God with life." In Job 21, Job refutes Eliphaz's premise with the same observation: "Why do the wicked live on, growing old and increasing in power? They see their children established around them. . . . Their homes are safe and free from fear. . . . They spend their years in prosperity and . . . say to God . . . 'Who is the Almighty, that we should serve him?'" *But* "their prosperity is not in their own hands," asserts Job (21:7–9, 13–16). Life is unfair, he insists. Trouble and death come to both the good and the bad in the end. Life is indeed unfair, but God is not. He is the just Judge—"he judges even the highest" (21:22). Job knows divine judgment is not fully meted out till after earthly life is ended. Yet he has the assurance that the Almighty has already judged and forgiven him, declaring him blameless.

Eliphaz, however, continues to push his point of view: "Is not your wickedness great? Are not your sins endless?" (Job 22:5).

Who needs a friend who comes by to tell us we've brought trouble on ourselves because of our sinfulness? Job helps himself by remembering that he serves a God of compassion and mercy. He understands that sin requires a sacrifice—someone to give his life's blood on behalf of another. He knows well enough that the wages of sin isn't suffering but rather death (Rom. 6:23). Yet Job had an amazing knowledge of God's mercy toward sinful people:

> I know that my Redeemer lives,
>> and that in the end he will stand upon the earth.
> And after my skin has been destroyed,
>> yet in my flesh I will see God;
> I myself will see him
>> with my own eyes—I, and not another.
> How my heart yearns within me!
>>> (Job 19:25–27)

Things are not made easy for Job, however, because Eliphaz, a man probably Job's senior, is one whose spirituality Job deeply respects. And Eliphaz applies additional pressure by citing a supernatural experience he has had. He claims that God has given him a message especially for Job. Here is what God "told" Eliphaz to tell Job:

> This truth was given me in secret, as though whispered in my ear. It came in a nighttime vision as others slept. Suddenly fear gripped me; I trembled and shook with terror, as a spirit passed before my face—my hair stood up on end. I felt the spirit's presence, but couldn't see it standing there. Then out of the dreadful silence came this voice: "Is mere man more just than God? More pure than his Creator?" (4:12–17, TLB)

Now, it's extremely difficult to say anything to someone who claims to have had such an experience and who links it with the message they deliver to you purportedly from the Lord! And yet we know that this man, though he may well have been sincere, was mistaken. At the end of the story, God says to Eliphaz, "I am angry with you . . . because you have not spoken of me what is right, as my servant Job has" (Job 42:7). Eliphaz had a theology of suffering that was seriously flawed, and Job, sick though he was, was able to discerns the error and reject it.

So often, when trouble comes, people say, "What have I done to deserve this?" as if something they have done has brought disaster down on their heads. While sometimes we do bring disaster by some of our sinful actions, *we could not possibly pay for our sin by any amount of suffering.* Sin is so serious that it can only be atoned for by the greatest sacrifice of all—death. And One, namely Christ our Redeemer, became our substitute, bearing our punishment and dying in our place. And so Job says boldly, "Now that I have prepared my case, I know I will be vindicated" (13:18).

Eliphaz rubs salt into Job's boils by urging him to be a better example. After all, Job is a leader, a model, the chief of his clan—the greatest man in all the East! He needs to do better, says Eliphaz. "In the past you have told many a troubled soul to trust in God and have encouraged those who are weak or falling, or lie crushed upon the ground or are tempted to despair. But now, when trouble strikes, you faint and are broken" (4:3–5, TLB). This is not at all a helpful thing to say to a Job. To add a burden of guilt about being a bad example (in Eliphaz's judgment) is something poor Job could do without!

To bear private grief publicly is something leaders often have to do, but an encouraging word might have been called for in this instance. Eliphaz could have chosen to commend Job for his faithful response to his wife or his refusal to curse God and die. This way his friend would have been built up rather than ground down. Job boldly begs his friends not to be "miserable comforters," but rather to "comfort the miserable":

> I have heard all this before. What miserable comforters all of you are. Won't you ever stop your flow of foolish words? What have I said that makes you speak so endlessly? But perhaps I'd sermonize the same as you—if you were I and I were you. I would spout off my criticisms against you and shake my head at you. But no! I would speak in such a way that it would help you. I would try to take away your grief. (16:2–5, TLB)

HOW TO LISTEN AND RESPOND

Do you respond, or react, to criticism? I must confess I usually react first and respond later, but I have learned some lessons along the way! First of all I ask myself, *Is it true?* Isaac D'Israeli said, "It's much easier to be critical than correct." If it's a correct criticism, try to humble yourself and own it. Then ask the Lord how to proceed in dealing with it. If it isn't true, you need to let it go rather than mull it over, rehearsing it late into the night or sharing it with friends on the phone, thereby keeping it alive.

Second, commit yourself to the Lord who judges fairly. After he had been judged by various people in varying degrees of hostility and accusation, the apostle Paul finally had to say, "It is a very small thing if I am judged by you." Sometimes we have to leave the record in God's hands, because we can't control what others think and what they say about what they think, and how many people they tell, and whether or not what they tell is true. Often, when we try to go back and clean up our record, it only muddies the waters.

Third, Paul urges us not to spend valuable time judging ourselves on the matter. If we have endless postmortems over a situation, no Kingdom work will ever get done! We need to take it to God and let His holy light into our hearts. We must open up the secret springs of our motivation for Him to examine, for He alone knows us through and through. Then as we commit our actions to His scrutiny, we need to rely on His judgment of the matter and, if it is possible, put right our part and leave the rest to Him.

Job found out that the one thing he needed to do above all else was to consider the source. Sometimes a critic is motivated by jealousy. Do you ever get the feeling that a person wants to see you fail or has some other spiritual ax to grind? So when someone says to you, "I have a word from the Lord for you," check it out against what you know about the person bringing you the message. Then check it against what you already know about God. And don't ignore what your own experiences of life have taught you. Job's general knowledge of life had enabled him to say, in essence, "Were you just born yesterday? Open your eyes! Good people have trouble all the time."

When Others Judge Who You Are

Bildad speaks next. He seems to be the amateur psychologist. His argument follows along lines similar to that of his friend Eliphaz, but he suggests that Job is not only reaping what he sows, he is no good as a person either. "Man . . . is but a maggot—a son of man . . . only a worm!" Bildad tells him (Job 25:6). Now, who needs enemies with friends like that? In effect, this friend is saying, "You are a disaster waiting to happen, not just because of what you have done. In fact, you've done what you've done because you are who you are! You're obviously worth nothing in God's eyes. You have no value as a person whatsoever." Many have been the recipients of such negative messages! Little children have been told by parents, "You're no good. You're not nearly as nice, as pretty or as smart as your sister." Or worse, "I wish you'd never been born." Many verbally abused children have grown up feeling like maggots because they have repeatedly been told by a "Bildad" that that's what they are! If you hear enough of that sort of talk, you may just begin to believe it. If Eliphaz has been a dominating friend, Bildad is a demeaning one. He attacks Job's personhood, telling him he is worthless and of little value. His verbal abuse appears several times—phrases that in today's vernacular would amount to "You are full of hot air" (Job 8:2) and "You shut up" (18:2).

Job responds by saying, "A despairing man should have the devotion of his friends" (6:14). To the charge that he is not worth anything, Job knows, as he has said to Eliphaz, "I'm worth redeeming! I know that my Redeemer lives." He assures himself—and reminds them—that God must see value in the one He redeems. What's more, Job knows that God even considers him worth glorifying: "In my flesh I will see God" (19:25–26).

When Job came out with his incredible statements of faith in chapter 19, he was drawing on his theology to help himself. He felt awful about his family, his friends and his health. Read Job 19:13–20 and find out how Job felt about the state of things. Everyone in his life was putting him down. But when others put him down, he let God build him up.

Whenever my self-worth is at a low point, I try to do what Job did. I tell myself, "Maybe people around me don't think I'm worth living for, but Jesus thinks I'm worth dying for! He's coming again—for me—and He's prepared a resurrection body, fit for a heavenly environment, where I will live with Him forever. He obviously thinks enough of me to raise me from the dead!" When people don't want to be around me—when I'm rejected, as Job was, by people I care deeply about—I remind myself *I'm accepted by Him*. These are things I know, and the knowing helps!

Bildad, however, has not only attacked Job's person but has added the cruelty of undeserved guilt. In chapter 8 he tries to draw a correlation between Job's lack of goodness and the deaths of his beloved children. "When your children sinned against him, he gave them over to the penalty of their sin" (Job 8:4). Not only had Job brought trouble on himself, but Bildad is implying that he had brought the sky down on his children's heads as well. In other words, Bildad is saying, "You weren't much of a father to your kids, Job. If you had been a godly dad, your children wouldn't have sinned against God and caused this catastrophe!" His words must have added greatly to Job's deep distress.

There is nothing that hurts more than the suggestion that something you have or have not done has resulted in harming the ones you love. Yet Bildad's cruel comment was clearly wrong. We are introduced to Job as he is praying fervently for his children. He was ever concerned with their spiritual well-being and, as priest of his clan, sacrificed regularly on their behalf. After their birthday celebrations, he would call them together for a worship time, in case they had "cursed God in their hearts." We read, "This was Job's regular custom" (1:5). Job was deeply concerned about his children's relationship with God, and to have Bildad suggest that what had happened to them had happened because of his flaws as a parent must have seared his soul. I can relate to receiving this kind of criticism.

Who Needs Enemies with Friends Like These?

When my husband used to travel extensively, I had no shortage of advice from my friends. I had well-meaning folks sympathize with my situation and send me sweet notes, encouraging Bible verses and veiled warnings of what might happen to the kids' faith if their dad continued to parent from a distance.

One day, returning home from the airport after seeing my husband off on a three-month tour of ministry, I was in a particularly low mood. I had invited a missionary friend to stay for part of the time and had just made us both a good pot of tea when there was a knock at the door. I opened it, and there stood Bildad!

The man I welcomed in to join our tea party was a family friend. He was an elder in our church, a wise brother in the Lord. He had been one of the men we had turned to for insight and guidance when we had left the business world and first gone into full-time Christian work. I respected him deeply and was delighted to see him. However, he soon came to the point of his visit. He told me he felt very strongly that Stuart should not continue to be an absentee father; it would affect the children. "How could he be a godly parent and fulfill his God-given role when he was away all the time?" he asked me.

I was shattered, struck dumb with fear. After all, those were the very worries of my own heart. What if he was right? And who was I to say that God had not sent him to warn us of the dire consequences of our lifestyle?

As I sat there, my teacup poised between the saucer and my mouth, our missionary friend spoke up. "You ask," she said respectfully but firmly, "how Stuart can fulfill the role of a father and be away all the time. I would ask you how can he fulfill the role of an evangelist and stay home all the time? There are some vocations in God's church that can't be done from home!" Bildad eventually left, and my friend and I talked far into the night. "You are modeling a sacrificial lifestyle for the children, Jill," my wise comforter said to me. "And you and Stuart are praying fervently for your little ones. They have such a rich, Christian heritage. They will be all right." She was right, as it happened. All our children serve the Lord today. But I spent a miserable three months worrying about it. One thing I decided: I would try not to be a Bildad in anyone else's life!

Job's third friend to speak is Zophar. If Eliphaz was dominating and Bildad was demeaning, Zophar is just plain discouraging! "Seeing you reap what you sow—suffering cannot be kept at bay," he says. Zophar is a determinist. Among other things he suggests that Job can't break the cycle of disaster or reverse the effects of the had choices that, Zophar believes, have brought trouble on Job. He even purports that God has forgiven some of Job's sins but not all of them. There must be some hidden habit that has Job by the throat, Zophar suggests.

But we know that the life of God in us, that is, the dynamic of the Spirit, can enable us to break the cycle of whatever dogs our spiritual footsteps. The message of the cross is that Jesus died and rose again to give us His power to overcome everything He overcame. "Sin shall not have dominion over you," Paul promised the Roman believers (Rom. 6:14, KJV). If Job had lived in another day and age, he would have borrowed Paul's wonderful words:

> No, in all these things we are more than conquerors through him who loved us. For I am convinced that neither death nor life, neither angels nor demons, neither the present nor the future, nor any powers, neither height nor depth, nor anything else in all creation, will be able to separate us from the love of God that is in Christ Jesus our Lord. (8:37–39)

Job sticks to his guns, refutes the arguments of his critics and appeals to God to hear his case. In turning resolutely to the Lord to give him the final word, not on the "why did it happen" of his dilemma but on the "how can I cope" of it, he begins to receive the help he needs. How can he hang in there to the end?

Likewise, how can we endure with patience the pain we are permitted to experience? How can we fathom the depth of the loving grace of God? How can we know God more fully and explain Him to our "friends"?

Without a friend in the world, Job discovered one in heaven, ready and willing to be the friend he needed.

What Does It Mean?

1. Review Revelation 12:9–10. Who is the source of criticism? Read First Peter 5:8 and Galatians 5:15. What are the similarities, and who is being talked about in each passage?

2. What was Eliphaz's argument in Job 4:7–8? Job's response is that life is hard for all people—that blessings come to both good and evil men. Read Psalm 73, written by Asaph. How does Asaph describe the wicked (73:8–15)? What is Asaph's reaction (73:2–5)? Where does he find some answers (73:17)? What does he learn about the wicked, and what does he learn about the godly (73:18–28)?

3. What was Bildad's argument in Job 25:1–6? Job's response is that we cannot save ourselves. Read Paul's statements in First Corinthians 15:9–10 and First Timothy 2:5–6. How do these passages confirm what Job believed before anyone had heard of Jesus Christ?

4. What was Zophar's argument in Job 11:5–6? If we believe that we've sinned so much that God can't even keep track of all of it—that He has only forgiven some of it—what hope do we have? Read Paul's answer to the Zophar argument in Ephesians 2:8.

5. How do you handle criticism from family and friends? Is there ever a time you should confront your "comforters" as Job confronted his? Explain.

6. Read Job 6:14–30. What does Job say about true friendship? What graphic picture does Job use to describe friends that fail (6:15–20)? Job says, "Now you too have proved to be of no help" (6:21). How can we avoid the same pitfalls when we try to be a comforter?

7. What is Bildad implying in Job 8:4? When are we responsible for our children's misfortunes—and when are we not?

8. Read First Corinthians 4:1–5. Who is getting after Paul? How does he handle criticism? Which part of this passage helps you, and why?

How Should I Pray?

- Pray for the "Eliphazes"—that our elders and leaders would have a balanced theology of suffering.

- Pray for the "Zophars"—that "salvation by works" teachers would discover grace, for themselves and for others.

- Pray that you and others in a position to criticize will be constructive critics.

- Pray that you and others in a position to give comfort will be wise comforters.

CHAPTER NINE

SOMEBODY'S PRAYING FOR ME

My witness is in heaven. . . . My intercessor is my friend.

JOB 16:19–20

We do not have a high priest who is unable to sympathize with our weaknesses, but we have one who has been tempted in every way, just as we are—yet was without sin. Let us then approach the throne of grace with confidence, so that we may receive mercy and find grace to help us in our time of need.

HEBREWS 4:15–16

PAIN creates an environment like an echo chamber where you can hear God's voice. C.S. Lewis said, "God whispers in our pleasures, speaks in our conscience, but shouts in our pain." But what does He shout? "I am your Redeemer!" I suppose if someone had asked Job what his life's verse was, he may well have said, "I know that my Redeemer lives." Elihu, the fourth friend who speaks, reminds Job that God has the power to redeem. It takes eternal power to give a person eternal life, and only the Eternal One can do it. He—the eternal God who has shown himself to Job—has somehow conveyed to Job that He has brought back his soul from destruction and He will not now abandon him or stop providing for him even when he is severely criticized.

Wouldn't Job have loved the Twenty-third Psalm! Job was a shepherd himself—he had seven thousand sheep! In his extremity, however, Job was beginning to doubt God's shepherding powers. Could God shield him from the mouth of the lion—in this instance, the sharp teeth of his friends' words? By now he is tempted to believe that God's provision in his pain is waning. Elihu cannot bear to see Job's fainting faith, and now joins in the discussion, with the intent of turning Job's eyes back to his Helper.

There is nothing like the pain of criticism. Elihu is quick to assure Job that it is not his intent to criticize. "Now, Job, listen to my words," he says at the beginning of Job 33. "I am just like you before God; I too have been taken from clay. No fear of me should alarm you, nor should my hand be heavy upon you" (33:1, 6–7). Elihu is telling Job, essentially, "I'm not here to get after you; rather, I'm here to affirm you." He becomes the advocate of God to Job and the three "miserable comforters." Elihu, on God's behalf, assures Job of the Lord's justice and knowledge. "I will ascribe justice to my Maker. . . . One perfect in knowledge is with you" (36:3–4). There is comfort in the omniscience and omnipresence of God, and Elihu knows it. So he tells Job he is right in his insistence that God, knowing his heart, has forgiven him. He is a just God and the Judge of all the earth—God will do the right thing.

When I am being roundly criticized, it helps when an Elihu comes along and reminds me that God perfectly and justly knows my heart because He lives right there in it!

THE JUDGE WHO MATTERS

Once the apostle Paul, like Job, was having trouble with some of his critics. The people after him were leaders—in Paul's case, leaders of the Corinthian church. Yet he boldly defended his ministry and motives, reminding those who were criticizing him that he was only a servant of Christ, yet a servant trusted with "the secret things of God." Paul told the Corinthians that his Master required him, as a good steward, to be faithful to his trust. Notice that the Master does not require us to be successful as the world defines success. He does not require us to be popular either—just faithful. If, as best as I know my heart, I have no known sin that is as yet unconfessed, and if I am doing my level best to serve Christ and people, then I can claim Paul's words and philosophy. I can do what both Elihu and Paul recommended. I can say, "I care very little if I am judged by you" (1 Cor. 4:3).

Notice that Job uses similar sentiments to Zophar in Job 12:2–3: "Doubtless you are the people, and wisdom will die with you! But I have a mind as well as you; I am not inferior to you." Job defends his standing before God and before men.

It's hard though, isn't it, when we are under the gun to care "very little" if we are judged? I usually care very much! But very much might well be too much. After all, it isn't other people (even important ones) or any human, worldly assessment that matters in the end—it is God who judges us. Paul points out, "He will bring to light what is hidden in darkness and will expose the motives of men's hearts. At that time [Judgment Day] each will receive his praise from God" (1 Cor. 4:5). Elihu reminds Job that God is a just judge, and He alone knows what a person is like on the inside. If we are first and foremost God pleasers, rather than people pleasers, we will be able to cast ourselves on God's merciful judgment and say, "Though all people forsake me, yet, Lord, I will continue to love and serve you."

CRITICISM FROM ALL SIDES

The devil loves to criticize. He started it all in the Garden of Eden, introducing the very first critical thought into God's perfect world. "Has God really said you shouldn't eat of the fruit?" he asked Eve, subtly suggesting that God must be an old spoilsport, unfair and unkind to withhold something so evidently pleasurable from them. Satan criticizes God to Eve and, after getting exactly what he wanted in the lives of God's children, thoroughly enjoyed hearing Adam begin to do Satan's work for him. When God asked Adam what he had done, eating the forbidden fruit, Adam answered, "The woman you gave me got me to do it!" So Adam criticized God for giving him Eve, and he criticized Eve for giving him the opportunity to sin! Whereupon, not to be outdone, Eve criticized the snake: "The serpent deceived me, and I ate." The spirit of ungodly criticism is from the pit of hell and is a destructive force in all our relationships.

And it doesn't stop with our relationships with others; some of the devil's greatest victories occur when he gets us to be our own destructive critics.

But aren't we called to examine our own hearts? Didn't David say, "Search me, O God, and know my heart" (Ps. 139:23)? There certainly is a spiritual self-judgment that is healthy, but some aspects of ourselves are beyond our ability to evaluate. There are some things that only God can fully understand, and so Paul says, "I do not even judge myself. My conscience is clear, but that does not make me innocent. It is the Lord who judges me. Therefore judge nothing before the appointed time; wait till the Lord comes" (1 Cor. 4:3–5).

"Wait till the Lord comes." It sounds so simple, but it may well be that some of us will be in God's waiting room until the second coming of Christ before the full story is ever told. Can we be content to leave it with God? Can we live with what we feel has been a personal failure, yet choose not to call it failure—or success—but leave the outcome and the evaluation with the God who sees it all clearly? Can we accept that a soured relationship may remain unresolved and that we may never know exactly what we said or did that contributed to the trouble? Coping with criticism—from within and without—begins with a willingness to not rehearse the details again and again but rather commit the whole thing to God and get on with our lives.

Of course it isn't only criticism of ourselves that takes the wind out of our sails. Sometimes the devil knows he can get to us far more effectively by criticizing those we love—our spouses or our children, for example. When people criticize Stuart, it's far harder for me to deal with than when they get after me! I wonder if Job's friends criticized Job's wife and her attitude? If they thought Mr. Job wasn't responding rightly to suffering, I've no doubt they didn't think much of Mrs. Job! I wonder how Job felt about that?

I have always struggled with this. I am a pastor's wife and so have had much opportunity to practice the right response to criticism! Shortly after becoming a pastor's wife, I found myself in a church meeting where my husband was the object of criticism. He sat there quietly, offering absolutely no defense. *Why doesn't he say something?* I wondered desperately. After a few more arrows aimed in his direction, I said to myself, *Well if he isn't going to defend himself I guess that is what a good Christian wife is for.* I rose to my feet, made an impassioned, one-minute speech, burst into tears and rushed from the auditorium! Since that traumatic event, I have done a little better at handling criticism. (*That wouldn't be hard*, I can hear you say.)

As a pastor's wife, it's difficult when people criticize you, but it's worse when they criticize your husband. Sometimes church members don't want to confront the pastor, but they feel they can pass on their complaints via the pastor's wife because she isn't so intimidating. Criticism takes many forms. "He's too deep," says one. "He's too shallow," says the next. "He's too dull. My kids are bored," confides another. Do they expect you to say, "Oh, I agree, Mrs. Smith, he bores me to pieces too"? Sometimes when I'm listening to someone criticize my husband, I think to myself, *Has this person forgotten I'm* **married** *to the man? How would she feel if I drew her aside by the coat racks to tell her I felt her husband really should smarten up his appearance?*

How do we handle such encounters? Perhaps we leap to our beloved's defense or cut the person off in mid-complaint. I usually feel quite sick or produce a migraine headache within half an hour of such an episode. After nearly forty-two years I still wrestle with the unfairness of it all. "They don't know how hard he worked on that sermon," I say to the Lord. Now, of course, if we find some truth in the criticism (and there is often some truth), we need to be mature enough to own that part of it and be teachable, pliable and changeable. Here are some of the ways I have learned to cope with criticism aimed at those close to me.

1. Hold your breath and count to twenty before saying anything at all.

2. Try to listen long enough to let complainers know they are being heard and that you have understood the problem.

3. As you listen, ask yourself why this person is so upset. Are they under pressure themselves from other quarters, and did your spouse (or whomever their complaint is about) happen along at the wrong moment? Often this is the case.

4. Let the first thing you say be a quiet and gentle word. "A soft answer turns away wrath" (Prov. 15:1, NKJV). "Thank you for being so concerned" is one possibility.

5. Try to be objective and impartial. Pretend, for the moment, that the one being criticized is not connected to you—almost impossible, but try anyway.

6. Don't start to reply with a defensive statement. Find a place to agree without being disloyal. For example, you could say, "I understand your children being bored in church, Mrs. Smith. Most children are at that age."

7. Quietly refute any criticism that is unfair or untrue with such statements as, "I'm not sure you've been given the whole story," or "If you knew all the circumstances, I think you'd judge the matter differently."

8. If you feel the criticism is justified, talk about it to the person who has been targeted. If not, don't mention it. No sense upsetting another person over accusations that are false.

9. Try to send complainers on their way with no new criticism of you!

We know that Job has had to deal with others' criticism of him. These same friends have implied that his children must have sinned, or they would not have been wiped out. And we can reasonably assume that his wife, who, in her grief, spoke like a foolish woman, has been assigned her share of the blame. Of Job's four friends, Elihu is the only one who does not join in this vicious cycle of blaming and judging. Notice that God does not include Elihu when He reprimands the other friends in chapter 42. He does not say Elihu spoke truly, but he does not say He did not speak truly as the others had done. We can learn from Elihu. When something does need to be said to our suffering friends, he can give us a clue as to what it should be.

A Friend in Heaven

If we would be an Elihu, the first thing we can do is remind Job that God is a just judge. The next thing we can do is remind him that though God is a judge, He is also a friend. Consider these wonderfully gentle words of comfort from Elihu: "He is wooing you from the jaws of distress to a spacious place free from restriction, to the comfort of your table laden with choice food" (Job 36:16).

What a helpful word for someone during hard times. In his distress Job had to be reminded of the gentle mercy and compassion of God.

Job is not hearing anything new here; Elihu is reminding him of an aspect of God that Job had discovered on his own, only much earlier. Back in 16:7 Job had been quite frank: "Surely, O God, you have worn me out; you have devastated my entire household." It was at this point that Job was still in danger of "confusing God with life." His friends could have used their tongues to bless rather than bite, but they did not. Job said to them, "Miserable comforters are you all! . . . I also could speak like you, if you were in my place; I could make fine speeches against you and shake my head at you. But my mouth would encourage you; comfort from my lips would bring you relief." Struggling to lift his eyes heavenward, Job came out with a profound affirmation of his faith in God: "Even now my witness is in heaven; my advocate is on high. My intercessor is my friend as my eyes pour out tears to God" (16:2, 4–5, 19–20).

Again, I am amazed at the revelation of God to this man. Didn't you think that the doctrine of the high priesthood of Jesus belonged to the book of Hebrews in the New Testament? What Job understood about all that God had told him, we have no way of knowing, but we do know from these verses that Job believed there was a witness in heaven who was his advocate, his intercessor and his friend! What is more, he believed that as he cried his heart out in deep, deep distress, this advocate pleaded with God for him "as a man pleads for his friend." Elihu had listened to all of this. Out of deference to the others' age and experience, he had said nothing. Now, twenty chapters or so later, Job needs Elihu to remind him of this One who cares for those who suffer as he, Job, is suffering.

Elihu also reminds Job that God is the great Music Maker. Elihu laments that no one says, "Where is God my Maker, who gives songs in the night?" (Job 35:10). God is just and holy, full of mercy, compassion and grace, but He is also the God of joy.

Habakkuk found that out after his own deep, dark time of trouble:

> Though the fig tree does not bud and there are no grapes on the vines, though the olive crop fails and the fields produce no food, though there are no sheep in the pen and no cattle in the stalls, yet I will rejoice in the LORD, I will be joyful in God my Savior. The Sovereign LORD is my strength; he makes my feet like the feet of a deer, he enables me to go on the heights. (Hab. 3:17–19)

God gave Habakkuk a song to sing when the Babylonians were running all over his life. "I will be joyful in God my Savior," he promises. Perhaps it was a song in a minor key, but who says that minor can't be lovely? God gave Hannah a song to sing when she had just given up her only, long-awaited and prayed for, son. She, who had been in bitterness of soul, sang, "My heart rejoices in the LORD" (1 Sam. 2:1). God gave Paul a song to sing as he sat in a dark, horrible prison for his faith in Jesus. He had every reason to give up, to curse God and die (better to die at His own hand than at the hand of the Romans), and yet he wrote that we are to "do everything without complaining or arguing, so that you may become blameless and pure, children of God without fault in a crooked and depraved generation, in which you shine like stars in the universe" (Phil. 2:14–15).

We are to shine like stars and sing like angels. Paul had just composed an incredible hymn extolling Christ's nature, work and exaltation, finishing with "that at the name of Jesus every knee should bow, in heaven and on earth and under the earth, and every tongue confess that Jesus Christ is Lord, to the glory of God the Father" (Phil. 2:10–11). When he wrote this exhortation to the Philippian church, he was in chains for the sake of the gospel. One can only sing such songs if one believes that God loves, God listens and God leads through the darkest of nights—that God is there, despite what all the circumstances seem to say to the contrary.

When others speak against us, God speaks for us; when others laugh at our misfortune, God weeps; when we are persecuted, the Lord Jesus shows us the wounds in His hands, His feet and His side; and when we doubt His ability to hold us fast, He tightens His grip. When we are, as Job puts it, "tossed to and fro in the storm," He stands up in our little boat and commands the winds and the waves to obey Him (Matt. 8:27). We can, as Job discovered, without hesitation and with confidence, depend on God to act on our behalf. Elihu encourages Job to put the emphasis on God's faithfulness and not on his own lack of faith. How can I be an Elihu to a Job? Help that Job focus on God's ability to sustain.

OUR ADVOCATE IN HEAVEN

Job would have found his dejection complete, apart from his tenacious faith. Elihu gave him some support, but it was God Himself who helped him to persist. The answer to Job's needs was not to be found in questioning his own heart actions or by doubting that God had forgiven him, but rather in trusting that his pain was not being treated with indifference in heaven. Though Job had few earthly friends, he believed he had one in heaven. "Even now," he reminds himself, "my witness is in heaven; my advocate is on high. My intercessor is my friend."

"Even now," Job is saying, with shining faith, "in the immediateness of my need, heaven debates my dilemma, and my advocate is taking my case right to the Supreme Court!"

Those two little words, "even now," have always been a great comfort to me. As I waited six hours in a hospital waiting room with one of our children who had broken her arm, I kept repeating that phrase, "even now." While the bureaucracy ground away (oh, so slowly) down here on earth, I believed that heaven was busy with our crisis.

On another occasion, I stood outside a rough place crowded with teenagers—many of them gang members—and I felt frightened and alone with all those wild young faces looking at me suspiciously. I breathed a prayer: "Even now—give me your words for these young people, Lord."

As I traveled down to Liverpool with a knot in my stomach to tell my widowed mother we were taking her beloved grandchildren and emigrating to America, I prayed, "Even now—Lord, help me tell her tenderly; it's so hard." And God gave us both grace to accept the parting.

As waves of homesickness engulfed me in those first few years in America, especially at Christmastime, I would glance heavenward and pray, "Help me relax in the knowledge that we are in the right place and that 'home' is the will of God—even now!" My friend Jesus in heaven pled with His Father on my behalf— "as a man pleads for his friends"—and I discovered that the heavenly Father always answers the prayers of His beloved Son!

Years ago, in my student days, I found myself without friends. I had just come to the Lord and had tried—unsuccessfully—to share my new faith with my few close friends. They were not impressed and blocked me out of any further relationship with them. In fact, my best friend, with whom I shared a small room, decided she would shut me out of her life completely and not even talk to me anymore. It's hard to do that when you are sharing a small space, but she managed. I had not yet discovered the world of new Christian friends waiting for me around the corner of my conversion, and I felt pretty lonely. I had just started to read my Bible and discovered the book of Hebrews. Because I had never read any of the Scriptures until then, Hebrews was probably not a very good place to start. Yet start I did, and at a pretty low place in my life—feeling abandoned by my closest associates. As I read, I discovered Hebrews 4:14–16:

> Therefore, since we have a great high priest who has gone through the heavens, Jesus the Son of God, let us hold firmly to the faith we profess. For we do not have a high priest who is unable to sympathize with our weaknesses, but we have one who has been tempted in every way, just as we are—yet was without sin. Let us then approach the throne of grace with confidence, so that we may receive mercy and find grace to help us in our time of need.

I didn't understand what it was all about, but I did grasp the single thought that I could count on a friend who could supply "grace to help in time of need." For the next few months, I learned to boldly enter the presence of God and talk my pain out. I got to know Jesus, my Advocate, in a way I perhaps would never have known Him if my friends had still been talking to me! I discovered, through my circumstances, that being a friend of Jesus is far more important than being a friend of anyone else. This was a lesson well learned at the very start of my Christian experience.

Even later, when God had brought me a world of friendships in the church, I was still learning that being a friend of Jesus was more important than being a friend of Jesus' friends! However good or bad my friends may be, in the words of a well-known hymn, "I dare not trust the sweetest frame, but wholly lean on Jesus' name." I could count on Him being my closest and best friend, even when clouds shielded His face and darkness hid His smile. Knowing that we have such a great High Priest—and such a friend—helps us to tighten our spiritual grip around the tenets of our faith. We know Jesus did not stay aloof from troubles but came to endure them too. He has walked where we walk, cried our tears, gone to our funerals and felt the betrayal and rejection of friends, disciples and family. Yet He responded rightly to suffering and "learned obedience from what he suffered" (Heb. 5:8). If the Lord Jesus can learn from His suffering, how much more can we learn from ours—especially when we know that Jesus is our advocate in heaven before God and the angels, and before the devil and all his accusations. Jesus prays for us. When we are pretty sure we don't have a friend in the world, we can know we have one in heaven. And what a friend! Yes, Elihu truly knew how to comfort Job. "God is a just Judge who sees your heart," he would say to us today, "but He is a loving, caring God as well."

What a Friend we have in Jesus,
All our sins and griefs to bear!
What a privilege to carry
Everything to God in prayer! . . .
Have we trials and temptations?
Is there trouble anywhere?
We should never be discouraged,
Take it to the Lord in prayer.[1]

What Does It Mean?

1. Jesus is our advocate in heaven. If we want to know what He is praying for us, we can read His prayer in John 17. Read John 17:20–26 and discuss or write about:

   • What is Jesus' concern in verses 20–23?

   • For whose sakes is He praying in verses 21–23?

   • Why should unity make such an impression on the world?

- Jesus asks for something stupendous for us in verse 24. What is it?

- Why will Jesus continue to make himself known to us (see verses 25–26)?

2. If Jesus is praying for us, why do we need to pray as well?

3. Jesus talked a lot about prayer. Make a list of the characteristics of hypocritical prayers and genuine ones from Matthew 6:5–8.

4. Remember C.S. Lewis said, "God whispers in our pleasures, speaks in our conscience, but shouts in our.pain." Has this been your experience? Share an example, or write about one in your journal.

5. Elihu speaks helpfully to Job, turning his eyes to the Lord and encouraging him not to become bitter. He says, "Those who suffer he delivers in their suffering; he speaks to them in their affliction" (Job 36:15). Read Psalm 23, Psalm 37:1–13 and Psalm 51, and discuss or write about how we could use these scriptures to encourage people.

6. Read Paul's prayer for the Philippians in Philippians 1:3–11 and his prayer for the Ephesians in Ephesians 1:15–23. Would you have liked Paul to be praying for you? Why or why not?

7. Read Job 16:19–21 and Hebrews 4:14–16. What did both Job and the writer of the Hebrews know about their Advocate in heaven? What did one record that the other didn't?

How Should I Pray?

- Praise God for all the people who have prayed for you through the years, starting with Jesus!

- Pray that your prayer work for others would mature like Paul's.

- Pray for the prayer ministry of your church.

- Borrow some phrases from Psalms 23, 37 and 51 to pray for people you know who need encouragement.

- Praise Jesus Christ for His work on our behalf as High Priest.

CHAPTER TEN

PERSISTING THROUGH PAIN

You have heard of Job's perseverance.

JAMES 5:11

As servants of God we commend ourselves in every way: in great endurance; in troubles, hardships and distresses; in beatings, imprisonments and riots; in hard work, sleepless nights and hunger; in purity, understanding, patience and kindness; in the Holy Spirit and in sincere love; in truthful speech and in the power of God; with weapons of righteousness in the right hand and in the left; through glory and dishonor, bad report and good report; . . . dying, and yet we live on; beaten, and yet not killed; sorrowful, yet always rejoicing; poor, yet making many rich; having nothing, and yet possessing everything.

2 CORINTHIANS 6:4–10

YEARS ago there was a little boy in a boarding school in Chefoo, China. His parents were far away; they were missionaries in the interior of that vast nation. One day war broke out between the Japanese and Chinese, and the Chefoo school was taken by the enemy. All the boys—hundreds of them—were moved out of the school compound and into a Presbyterian compound, which was much larger. Here, along with other expatriates, businessmen and sundry foreigners, the boys, under the care of their missionary teachers (also captives), tried to normalize their lives.

Far away, separated by the wild terror of the ongoing war between China and Japan, the mother of that boy heard what had happened. Suddenly she found herself in a "Job" situation. She also found herself in God's waiting room. She wanted to stop all she was doing and pray. She was tempted to quit her work of guiding a small group of believers and just hammer on heaven's doors for help. Instead, she continued fulfilling her responsibilities. In her words, the Lord said to her, "You look after the things that are precious to Me, and I'll look after the things that are precious to you!" Able to wait on the Lord and not on the answers to her agonized prayers for her children, she labored on. She persisted. God did take care of what was precious to her; little J. Hudson Taylor III survived his imprisonment and lived out many years of ministry in China.

The pain of waiting gives us a marvelous chance to grow some flowers of persistence in our lives. This is because waiting for the pain to pass gives us an opportunity to get into some spiritual action. But people don't persist these days—or so it seems to me. It takes so little to change their minds.

I have found it frustrating, for example, to set up a meeting to organize an event or do some practical ministry of service. Perhaps we need to bag groceries for the poor, babysit in the church nursery or stuff envelopes for a church mailing. Too often I find that only half (and sometimes not even half) the people who sign up to help show up! And I really think it's getting worse.

On one occasion a lady bought craft materials for twelve women in her church. They were to make one item for themselves and one to sell for missions. She went to all the trouble of buying and arranging the materials, readying her house and preparing refreshments for all the women who had signed up saying they would come, only to have not one of them show up. As you can imagine, she was not a little discouraged. So she called each person to find out why they hadn't come. The excuses were exceedingly weak, to say the least! The most frequent one was, "Oh, I changed my mind." People don't show up anymore!

If we can't follow through on our commitment to a craft class for missions, I wonder if we'll be able to follow through when the going really gets difficult. The book of James tells us that Job's perseverance became legendary. It is an example, says the apostle, to all of us.

> Brothers, as an example of patience in the face of suffering, take the prophets who spoke in the name of the Lord. As you know, we consider blessed those who have persevered. You have heard of Job's perseverance and have seen what the Lord finally brought about. The Lord is full of compassion and mercy. (James 5:10–11)

Persistence doesn't involve merely what we do but our very character. A person who has built this trait into his or her life will likely follow through when the hard times come. In looking at Job's reflections on his own life, we see patterns of persistence that made it possible for him to weather the storms. This trait shows up in three areas of his life.

PERSISTENCE IN MARRIAGE

We have had a small glimpse of the agony of Job's wife and her reaction to the suffering they were both enduring. She wasn't doing very well at all. Suffering can pull couples apart or drive them together. I am told the divorce rate for couples who have children with serious medical disorders is exceptionally high. And remember, tragedy had struck not one but ten of their children.

But Job has set up a solid pattern in his marriage: "I made a covenant with my eyes not to look lustfully at a girl" (Job 31:1). He is conscious that God wants him to be faithful to the wife of his youth. "Does [God] not see my ways and count my every step?" he asks (Job 31:4). Furthermore, Job claims that he is innocent of being unfaithful in any sense. "If my heart has been led by my eyes, or if my hands have been defiled, then may others eat what I have sown, and may my crops be uprooted. If my heart has been enticed by a woman, or if I have lurked at my neighbor's door, then may my wife grind another man's grain, and may other men sleep with her. For that would have been shameful, a sin to be judged" (31:7–11). What words! Job had made a covenant with his wife and a covenant with his eyes and claims to have kept it! He persisted. Any deviation would, he says emphatically, be "a sin to be judged." Job persisted in his marriage in spite of his wife's emotional estrangement. "My breath is offensive to my wife," Job laments, giving us a clue that his illness had alienated not only his relatives, colleagues and friends, but also his own spouse.

Not long ago my husband and I were listening to a couple who was having severe difficulties in their marriage. Stuart reminded them about the covenant they had made with each other years before. They had made that covenant before God and witnesses. They had promised to be faithful to each other, God helping them, till death parted them. He then reminded them that a promise like that need to be lived out on a moment-by-moment basis. "How do I do that?" one of them wanted to know. "You make a daily covenant with your eyes," I suggested. "Your eyes are the gate to your heart. Promise God and yourself that you will not allow them to look lustfully at another person." King David, walking on the roof of his house, saw a beautiful woman, Bathsheba, taking a bath. The first look wasn't sin, but the second and third were, and the situation ended in disaster and death. As an old Chinese proverb has it, "You can't stop the birds flying over your head, but you can stop them nesting in your hair!" Job persisted in his faithfulness to his wife.

My husband suggested to the young couple that if both of them would determine to keep their covenant to each other, then no matter how bad their relationship was, there was hope. "It's a bit like you being caught up in a fire in a burning building," he explained. "At this point I see both of you standing among the flames with a key in your hand. The key is to the fire escape. Yet you promised each other years ago you would throw that key—that option out of the situation—out the window. If you'll stop trying to cut a new key, you'll be able to give all your energy to putting out the flames instead!"

Persistence is patience. Patience is love waiting out a particularly painful situation. Job had persistently stuck to his wife. Job loved his wife, really loved her. Real love—God's love—is characterized by being primarily concerned with your beloved's well-being, regardless of the cost to yourself or the reaction of the one so loved. The Hebrew word for God's love is *hesed*. Covenants—marriage promises—are broken because people try to use their own inadequate human love and don't use the power of *hesed* when this human love runs out. This love of God is our power to suffer a situation longer than we think we can—to persist when we want out. Job was "in it" for life—till death parted them, not divorce. In the end his persistence paid off. He and his wife are still together at the end of the story.

PERSISTENCE IN PARENTHOOD

In the first glimpse we are given of Job in chapter 1, we are introduced to him as a father. Apparently he and his wife had ten children—seven sons and three daughters. These siblings obviously enjoyed each other. As wealthy young princes and princesses, heirs to their father's fortune, they met together to have fun! To feast and laugh together. Whenever there was half an occasion, they used it as an excuse for a big party that could well go on for days. Job 1:4 says, "His sons used to take turns holding feasts in their homes, and they would invite their three sisters to eat and drink with them." Job was the patriarchal and priestly head of his family. He was also leader and priest of his clan. The Bible says, "When a period of feasting had run its course, Job would send and have them purified. Early in the morning he would sacrifice a burnt offering for each of them, thinking, 'Perhaps my children have sinned and cursed God in their hearts.' This was Job's regular custom" (1:5).

Job prayed for his children. He persisted in prayer for them as a regular custom. Persistence means that we do something regularly. He had an awful dread that one of them might sin. He labored on for them, pleading with God for purity of heart and mind and a godly lifestyle. It was important to Job that his kids lived what they believed. He patiently and persistently persevered in his parenting. He wanted to bring those children up in the nurture and admonition of the Lord.

Persistent patience with your kids doesn't mean being patient with any old thing! Godly patience means we patiently see to it, as best we know how, that our children do the right thing. That they don't give up. That they "keep on keeping on" and learn persistence too.

PERSISTENCE IN MINISTRY

Suffering can disrupt a ministry. Sometimes it's hard getting back into the swing of things after a long layoff through illness or for other reasons. Other people often fill in for us or take over altogether, and it's difficult to get people to come back to you when you return. Now, Job had had a wonderful ministry before trouble came calling. We can read about that in chapter 29:

I rescued the poor who cried for help,
    and the fatherless who had none to assist him.
The man who was dying blessed me;
    I made the widow's heart sing.
I put on righteousness as my clothing;
    justice was my robe and my turban.
I was eyes to the blind
    and feet to the lame.
I was a father to the needy;
    I took up the case of the stranger.
I broke the fangs of the wicked
    and snatched the victims from their teeth. . . .
Men listened to me expectantly,
    waiting in silence for my counsel.
After I had spoken, they spoke no more;
    my words fell gently on their ears.
They waited for me as for showers
    and drank in my words as the spring rain.
When I smiled at them, they scarcely believed it;
    the light of my face was precious to them.
I chose the way for them and sat as their chief;
    I dwelt as a king among his troops;
    I was like one who comforts mourners.
                (Job 29:12–17, 21–25)

Job reminisces over the good old days when "I was in my prime, when God's intimate friendship blessed my house" (29:4). He talks of going to "the gate of the city and [taking his] seat in the public square" (29:7). This refers to the place where leaders gather to rule and make policy for the population. Job was a leader of leaders; certainly he was the one considered governor of his region. When he would take his seat of public office in the city gates, he tells us, "the young men saw me and stepped aside and . . . the chief men refrained from speaking and covered their mouths with their hands" (29:8–9). Job was held in high regard.

Then come words that tell the difference once Job returned home from his ash heap and tried to begin again. "But now," he says, "they mock me, men younger than I, whose fathers I would have disdained to put with my sheep dogs. . . . I have become a byword among them. They detest me and keep their distance; they do not hesitate to spit in my face. . . . Have I not wept for those in trouble?" he asks. "The churning inside me never stops; . . . I stand up in the assembly and cry for help" (30:1, 9–10, 25, 27–28).

What a difference! Before, his audience had hung on every word that came out of his mouth; now they stay away in droves, only coming near him "to spit in my face." But Job keeps going; he persists. He stands up to be laughed at—and even reaches out to those who spit in his face.

He persists! He knows he is responsible only for his attitude, not anyone else's, and he patiently waits on the Lord to turn the situation around. To keep on giving when no one takes; to keep on teaching when hardly anyone comes to hear; to keep on trying to lead when no one is following—that takes persistence and patience: the patience of Job!

Persistence that Pays Off

I am writing this chapter in Brasilia, in the heart of the great nation of Brazil. We have come at the invitation of Wycliffe Bible Translators to minister at their missions conference. Some of these people have spent forty years living with Indians in the vast Amazon rain forest or in other areas, trying to learn the various and difficult tribal languages. Then, having learned them, they translate the New Testament so the people can have the Word of God in their heart language. The Bible is available in Portuguese, but many of these tribal people don't know Portuguese. This job takes the patience of Job. Add to that a cool reception to the whole project by government officials and many of the Indians themselves, and you can guess what kind of dogged determination it takes to keep on keeping on!

Al, a veteran long-term missionary, told me many stories of the discouragements awaiting someone who goes uninvited to one of these groups and begins from scratch, trying to understand sounds and words that no one from the outside world has ever heard or written down. "They didn't want my wife and me to stay," he told me. "Many nights they would burn the boards on the roof of our makeshift house. We would replace them. They threatened our lives," he said. They loved on. Al would follow the Indians to the fields day after day with his tape recorder, recording the sounds of this strange tongue, because the Indians refused to assist or become language helpers. The couple persevered, even when the Indians told Al they didn't want their language written down.

One night Al was sleeping in a donkey barn—the only place they would let him stay. He was exceedingly discouraged. "Do you want me to stay, Lord? What am I doing here?" he asked. Maybe it was the fact that he was sleeping in a donkey barn that brought the passage to mind, but he remembered the story in the Gospels about Jesus sending for a donkey so he could ride it into Jerusalem. *Well*, Al thought, *even though I feel like an ass, I guess God needs me to carry Jesus to these people just like the donkey carried Jesus into Jerusalem—a city that turned against Him.* So he and his wife persisted. They stayed and prayed and loved and listened to the strange sounds. Today a ministry that people rejected has been received, and the New Testament has been written in their heart language.

We give up far too easily when people do not receive our message of life. Like many of us, Job found out that home is so often the last place that will receive a message from us about the

Lord. But God wants us to endure to the end. He wants us to show up and keep it up till He says to our spirit, "That's enough; well done, good and faithful servant!" Job was a servant leader and it takes a lot of perseverance to "serve one another in love" (Gal. 5:13).

Many years ago I was teaching a women's Bible study group. I had painstakingly visited all the houses around our own, inviting the older women who were my neighbors to come to a Bible study at our house. After weeks of visiting, three people showed up. They were all well into their seventies. It was hard going. It took so much time and energy to prepare a lesson, get a babysitter so I could go and pick up the women, have the study and serve them refreshments, and then get a babysitter so I could take them all home!

One day one of the women got sick and one quit coming. That left me with one! It was hard to persist, to patiently wait it out, to work as hard preparing my lesson for one as I would have worked for one hundred. But I knew God was expecting me to be faithful with that one woman, not only for her sake (she eventually came to Christ), but also for mine. We need opportunities to practice patience. If we get ourselves out of all the irritating, discouraging situations in order to relieve tension and stress, how will we ever grow endurance? I am so glad I persisted, even though, like Job, my stomach would often churn inside, especially when I would go to all that trouble, and my one woman was sick and hadn't bothered to let me know! One day God began to bring me other women in the neighborhood, and I was soon surrounded with a crowd to teach—just as Job was in chapter 42 at the end of his story. So Job grew the flower of persistence in the garden of his marriage, his parenting and his ministry.

Take a minute and think about the particular situation that is giving you an opportunity to practice patience. Try to hunker down for the long haul and wait it out with dogged determination if you can. Then, like Job, you may become an example and encouragement to others who are in trying situations too. James 5:11 says, "As you know, we consider blessed those who have persevered. You have heard of Job's perseverance and have seen what the Lord finally brought about." If we learn to persevere, others will point to our example and be helped. They will hear about our endurance and take heart.

One thing that helps us while we are hanging around being patient is to practice praise. We have already talked a little about how praise helps us when we are in pain, but it bears repeating because praise takes our eyes off ourselves and fastens them on God—and He, after all, is our great and glorious example of perseverance.

Jesus persisted in Nazareth. He was a carpenter for thirty years, patiently working well below His potential, which takes commitment! That must have been frustrating to have to make tables or chairs, or perhaps build a house, when he had built the universe. (In Proverbs 8:30 God calls Him "the craftsman at his side" in creation.)

He persisted in ministry when He was popular and when He was persecuted. "Even in his own land and among his own people, the Jews, he was not accepted. Only a few would welcome and receive him" (John 1:11–12, TLB), but He came, knowing they wouldn't receive Him, and He died for them anyway! That takes persistence. He persisted in loving the loveless, helping the helpless, and taking on the opposition in the name of truth.

And His Holy Spirit persists today—convicting people of sin, convincing them that Jesus is the answer to their need and converting enemies into friends. That takes persistence. But then Paul tells us in First Corinthians 13 that love—that sort of love—never fails. That doesn't mean it never fails to bring a response; it means God's love never fails to go on loving whatever the response! For this sort of self-giving love we need Jesus—and for this we have Jesus!

When you can't praise God for what He allows, try praising Him for who He is in the middle of what He allows. The love of God is poured into our hearts by the Holy Spirit, and He is the Spirit of perseverance! A friend who serves the Lord in France and has seen her hard-won converts falling by the wayside, moving out of the area or just becoming so discouraged they stopped coming to the mission altogether, keeps on keeping on. "So who is He for you, Cathy?" I asked her. "He's wonderful," she replied, her eyes shining. "He's so wonderful it doesn't even matter that everything is so dreadful. I can praise Him for who He is even in this mess!" If we are oriented to performance and results, it's hard to remember that obedience—faithfulness and persistence—is all He asks of us. Praise helps us remember that.

Praise helps us to stop worrying so much about the outcome. It helps us trust Him more. It reminds us God is big enough, strong enough and loving enough to sustain and help—even when we feel useless. Praise lifts our lagging spirits. In fact, Isaiah tells us God will give us "the oil of gladness instead of mourning, and a garment of praise instead of a spirit of despair" (Isa. 61:3).

Chuck Swindoll writes about pain being "one of the few things we all have in common. Maybe," he says, "you are the one with the crushed spirit right now—the hidden heartache that is too deep for words and too private for prayer chains."[1] If this is so, ask God to use pain positively in your life to grow the beautiful and fragrant flower of persistence.

Spend time in James 5:10–12, and ask God to work in your heart a mighty enabling to endure.

What Does It Mean?

1. Read chapter 3 of Job to get a feeling for how pain is affecting Job. What sort of pain is he suffering? Read chapters 4 and 5. Which sort of pain is hardest for you to handle?

2. Share or write about examples (famous or personal) of someone who has persisted in living well in the midst of pain.

3. Read James 1:2–4. How can we consider this "pure joy"? Be honest!

4. What sort of pain did the Lord Jesus deal with in others?
   - Matthew 9:1–8
   - Matthew 9:27–29
   - Matthew 9:32–33
   - Matthew 11:28

5. What sort of pain did the Lord Jesus deal with in His own life?
   - Matthew 13:53–58
   - Matthew 26:39–45
   - Matthew 27:32–50
   - Mark 9:14–19
   - John 11:32–36

6. Read Isaiah 53 and meditate or reflect in writing upon verses 10–12.

How Should I Pray?

Praise God for:
- what He knows of pain
- His persistence through pain

Pray for:
- the sick
- the elderly
- refugees
- the homeless
- those suffering for their faith
- war victims
- the lonely and depressed
- people in pain who don't know Christ
- people in pain who do know Christ
- people who need to know how Jesus suffered and died for them.

CHAPTER ELEVEN

OUT OF THE STORM AND INTO HIS ARMS

Then the LORD answered Job out of the storm.

JOB 38:1

*Then Peter got down out of the boat, walked on the water and came toward
Jesus. But when he saw the wind, he was afraid and, beginning to sink,
cried out, "Lord, save me!" Immediately Jesus reached out his hand and
caught him. "You of little faith," he said, "why did you doubt?"*

MATTHEW 14:29–31

THE writings of C.S. Lewis have enjoyed a lasting popularity
with people of faith, and they have challenged and inspired
people still in search of faith. One of his collections is called *God
in the Dock*. A dock is the term we use in Great Britain for "witness stand." Lewis points out that God is not on trial, however
much we human beings like to try to put Him in "the dock" and
cross-examine Him. Rather, we are the ones on trial. We are "in
the dock." One of the ways we can survive suffering is to rest
from our constant questioning and try to hear the Lord's voice
out of our particular storm. What questions is He asking us?

> Then the LORD answered Job out of the storm. He said:
> "Who is this that darkens my counsel with words without
> knowledge? Brace yourself like a man; I will question you,
> and you shall answer me." (Job 38:1–3)

In the beginning of his troubles, Job asks God, "Why, if You knew what terrible things would happen to me, did You ever allow me to be born?" Job asks God many other questions during the course of his trials, but toward the end of the story the roles become reversed, and God begins to question Job.

Most of us know the story about Peter walking on the water. When he and some other disciples were on the Sea of Galilee and a storm arose, they were terrified. They were seasoned enough sailors to recognize that they were in severe danger. Their fear, however, was heightened when they saw what they supposed to be a ghost, walking on the water toward them.

Jesus (for it was He, and no apparition) calmed their fears. Peter was so encouraged that he decided to leave the boat and walk on the water himself. But he began to watch the winds and waves instead of watching Jesus. As the disciple began to sink into the sea, Jesus said to him, "You of little faith, why did you doubt?" (Matt. 14:31).

In the same way, God walks over the waves that are about to capsize Job's small vessel of faith; He comes alongside and, as Job's emotions are being tossed around all over the place, says, "You've asked me quite enough questions—now it's my turn. O you of little faith . . . why ever did you doubt?" It's hard to answer that question when God asks it, but it must be done. Why do we doubt? Why do we waver?

I remember facing a storm of separation. We had been invited to immigrate to America in order to serve Elmbrook Church in Wisconsin. I had to tell my recently widowed mother. I remember driving very slowly down to Liverpool in order to break the news to her. I cried all the way there, stammered through my information, hugged my beloved "Peggy," and cried all the way home again.

On the way down, all I could hear were the winds; all I could see were the waves. I knew Jesus was there, encouraging me, but

I could hardly see Him through my tears. It was hard enough to try to cope with the storm of my own emotions at such a time, but I knew that my news would bring a tempest down on my own mother's head—one she could well do without at that particular time.

As I drove home again, I thanked the Lord for helping me to tell her and for letting her see the deep pain our parting would bring to me. I had honestly feared I could not do this to her—that I couldn't find the words—that she and I, together, would sink in the tempest of our grief. I thought of Jesus' words to Peter: "You of little faith, why did you doubt?" What had I doubted? I had doubted I could tell her, doubted we could survive the pain of parting, doubted that God could bring us both to acceptance and peace. I had even doubted He would get in the boat with us and still the storm in our hearts. On that long drive home up the English motorway, I could still hear the wind, and my eyes kept wandering to the waves; but now I sensed His arm under my elbow, guiding my feet over all I had been sinking under. Some partings have to be, but one parting never has to be. Nothing can part me from Jesus!

James addresses this subject of doubt in his letter to the believers of his day, who were facing many trials. "Perseverance must finish its work so that you may be mature and complete, not lacking anything." Then James says that if any of you don't understand what is happening and why the test is testing you—if you lack wisdom—you should ask God the right questions, and He will give you the right answers. Such a person should ask questions like, "How on earth can I consider this trial 'pure joy,' Lord?" or "Is this test doing what You want it to do in my life, Father—namely, to develop my character and grow endurance so that I can be a mature believer and walk through the storm?" (James 1:2–5).

LAYING OUR QUESTIONS DOWN

If I have questions for God, they need to be the right ones, and I need have no doubt whatsoever that God will answer me and tell me what I need to know and do in order to tap into His power to endure. What I will certainly need to learn is to trust Him more and not less, to stop depending on my feelings, and to develop my faith. And what I must ask the Lord is, "What do I say to others who question me about my misfortunes?" If I ask God these sorts of questions, I can have every assurance that He will answer me.

It's quite all right to ask God any question under the sun, but there are questions we need to ask in order to proceed with our lives. If we can dare to seek God's help in asking the hard questions, He will direct us to some things that will maximize the blessings suffering can bring to us. For example, we can ask Him, "How can this trouble You have permitted make me more like You?" instead of "Why aren't You removing this trouble?" God listens to every word we say, and we mustn't doubt His eager attention.

But if I doubt He's even there, that He's listening or that He is interested in making a wise person out of me in the middle of the mess, then I will be "like a wave of the sea, blown and tossed by the wind. That man," says James, "should not think he will receive anything from the Lord; he is a double-minded man, unstable in all he does" (James 1:7–8).

It's easy to feel as if our little craft of faith is being tossed about like a cork in the storm, isn't it? Job felt just like that. Yet, when the storm was at its height, God spoke to Job above the sound of the tempest and asked him why he had a problem with the problem!

Chapters 38 through 42 are glorious chapters. After an uncanny silence, Job at last hears the voice he has been longing to hear. After seeing nothing—he sees God! And, hearing and seeing, he worships in a way he has never worshiped before. He lays his questions down at the feet of the Lord and kneels there, stunned in wondering abandonment. "My ears had heard of you but now my eyes have seen you," he cries (Job 42:5).

Ruth Bell Graham is a wonderful poet. I love to read her work. One of her poems particularly caught my eye:

> I lay my "whys" before Your Cross
> in worship kneeling,
> my mind too numb for thought,
> my heart beyond all feeling.
> And worshipping,
> realize that I
> in knowing You
> don't need a "why."[1]

Elihu had tried to get Job to lay his questions down, to lift his eyes to God and His faithfulness, and not to concentrate on his own lack of faith. God is about to demand of Job how he could possibly have doubted His ultimate care for him when the evidence of His care for lesser creatures was all around him. First, he reminds Job in chapter 38 that He is the Creator and Job is the creature:

- "Where were you when I laid the earth's foundation?" (38:4)
- "Have you ever given orders to the morning, or shown the dawn its place?" (38:12)
- "Have you journeyed to the springs of the sea or walked in the recesses of the deep?" (38:16)
- "Have you comprehended the vast expanses of the earth? Tell me, if you know all this." (38:18)
- "Have you entered the storehouses of the snow?" (38:22)
- "Can you bind the beautiful Pleiades?" (38:31)
- "Can you loose the cords of Orion?" (38:31)
- "Can you bring forth the constellations in their seasons or lead out the Bear with its cubs?" (38:32)

I can imagine that Job, confronted with the incredible majesty of God, displayed in the thunderstorm that drenched his blackened and diseased skin and plastered his rags to his body, is devastated by those questions. "Will the one who contends with the Almighty correct him?" God asks Job. "Let him who accuses God answer him!" No wonder Job says, "I am unworthy—how can I reply to you? I put my hand over my mouth. I spoke once, but I have no answer—twice, but I will say no more" (40:2–5).

Then the Bible says the Lord spoke to Job out of the storm.

EVIDENCE OF GOD'S CARE

Where can we go when we are in trouble? We can walk out our front door into this, our Father's world. We can see His fingerprints. We can climb a mountain, walk an ocean shore and hear the waves pound beside us. We can stand in a downpour or watch the stars on a clear night. We can play in the snow and realize, as Job did, our "dust-ness," our infinitesimal size and, in contrast, become aware of the awesome ability of our Creator! God sees fit to remind Job of his humble origins. Dust he is and to dust he will return, but Job is dust dignified by Divinity, indwelt by the Spirit, and he will live again! It will take the might of a creative, awesome God to raise him from the dead, but Job is exposed to God in action in nature, and he is convinced.

God gives Job some answers to his questions from other creatures in the creation. It is God, the one who formed the lions, ravens, mountain goats and wild donkeys, who also made Job. God provides the animals, birds and reptiles with food and attends the birth of their young (38:39–39:4). What is more, He is stronger than the strongest creature—even the ox—and swifter than the ostrich or the stork. When the stork spreads her feathers to run, she laughs at the horse and rider, says the Lord. God made the horse to charge and the eagle to soar. Cannot He, who counts every egg in every bird's nest and mourns their loss, count the tears Job has cried and care for his sorrow over the loss of his young? How can even the whisper of a doubt about God's just doings dare to come from Job's lips?

God also points out that Job knows very little about the government of the spiritual realm—the sphere of life and death (38:33; 40:9–14). Like the mighty hippopotamus and cruel crocodile with their incredible, fearsome strength—both monsters— the monsters of life and death are under God's control. God is able to humble the mighty lumbering mammoths of the swamps as surely as He is able to humble "every proud man" and "crush the wicked where they stand" (40:12). Job is not up to such god-like work, for his arm is too short to save sorrowful sinners.

Job can answer nothing to this. He is ashamed of his doubts, his fears that God—this God of majesty, power, grace and provision—had abandoned him. He realizes he must never dictate how God must use His sovereignty. How does Job dare to suggest the times and seasons of his misfortunes or his blessings? Job sees himself as unworthy of God's grace. There is no trace of resentment or anger left. It is enough that God loves and cares for him. Seeing God, Job subjects all he is and has to Him and begins to serve Him again.

If suffering is a megaphone, it is also a magnifying glass. "My ears had heard of you, but now my eyes have seen you!" says Job (42:5). Elihu has warned Job, "The godless in heart harbor resentment" (36:13), and Job must have been reminded of his own rebuke to his wife. She was talking like a godless woman, and now he has been in danger of thinking like a godless man. Elihu has been right in charging Job with the lack of a proper response to the blessings misfortune brings. He responds again with faith and perseverance, and resolves to avoid all bitterness. A bitter spirit blocks all hope of help and comfort.

FINDING GOD IN ISOLATION

One thing I have learned from Job is not to fear the isolation that suffering so often brings. One gets the feeling that Job is absolutely alone with God in these closing chapters of his book. If only we can celebrate that possibility and stop being bitter at our friends and their inadequate efforts to comfort us. If we can take opportunities to spend more time alone with Him, we will see God, and we can begin to have a Job-chapter-42 experience.

I think of the Chinese pastor who gave his testimony at an international convention. He had been mistreated for his faith and put in a prison camp. Because of his resilient spirit and persistent faith and testimony, he was assigned to clean the cesspool. From morning till night, he stood in human waste. He was quite alone, for obvious reasons, but he chose to believe he was alone for divine reasons too! Here he could talk to God, sing songs and listen to his Lord without fear of repercussions. There was nowhere in the rest of the prison camp quite like that!

"Do you want to know my favorite song of praise?" he asked that great congregation. Without waiting for an answer, he began to sing:

> I come to the garden alone,
> While the dew is still on the roses;
> And the voice I hear, falling on my ear,
> The Son of God discloses.
> And He walks with me, and He talks with me,
> And He tells me I am His own,
> And the joy we share as we tarry there,
> None other has ever known.
>
> He speaks, and the sound of His voice
> Is so sweet the birds hush their singing,
> And the melody that He gave to me,

Within my heart is ringing.
And He walks with me, and He talks with me,
And He tells me I am His own,
And the joy we share as we tarry there,
None other has ever known.[2]

Our Chinese brother did not question the sovereignty of God in allowing him to come to this dreadful place. He thought rightly about God and spoke truly of His ways to all his fellow prisoners and his guards. He told his captors what Joseph told his brothers: "You intended to harm me, but God intended it for good!" (Gen. 50:20). He praised God for the good he could see in his terrible situation—that good being his isolation and, therefore, his opportunity to spend time with God alone, a privilege everyone else in the camp was denied.

There in the cesspool he praised God day after day. He insisted on believing that his God was at work out of sight and gave thanks for the good that would come, according to the mystery of God's divine will. The disproportionate amount of suffering that was permitted to come to him did not stunt his faith, and whereas his plans had, humanly speaking, gone sadly awry, he believed with Job that no plan of God could be thwarted—by his jailers, the communist government or by the very devil himself.

Like Job, this pastor was able to say, "I know that my Redeemer lives," and "He lives in me and for me and for His greater glory." Do you find yourself in a cesspool? Is it a cesspool that has caused everyone to stay away from you? Perhaps this was the only way God could get your attention! Maybe we need to visit Gethsemane and see Jesus alone, praying into the night for our souls. We need to hear the disciples' snores and realize that God knows the doubtful privilege of such "miserable comforters" firsthand. We need to see the angel comforting and strengthening the isolated Savior for the horrendous task ahead. When Jesus was drowned in the cesspool of our sins at Calvary, He was drowned alone. Unlike in Job's situation, even His Father was absent! How can we doubt that such a one as this loves us and understands?

Years ago, in a trial that had been permitted to come to me, I wrote:

> Help me accept the trials allowed—
> My losses and my troubles,
> Help me accept that life is not
> A pretty bowl of bubbles.
> Help me remember there's no
> Empty tomb without a tree,
> That Jesus wouldn't save Himself
> But died to set me free—
> Help me when crying on my bed,
> To know You count my tears
> Have planned my moments and my days,
> And brooded o'er my years—
> And so I ask Your help, dear God
> To bear the pain life gives,
> Endure with joy my darkest hour,
> For my Redeemer lives!

What Does It Mean?

1. Share briefly or write about one of the worst storms of your life. God spoke to Job out of the storm (Job 38:1–4). How can we help ourselves to hear His voice above the noise? Share some practical answers.

2. Storms come to us in many shapes and sizes. Look up the following incidents:

- Numbers 21:4–9
- 2 Kings 4:1–7

What was the storm, and how was it stilled?

3. Jonah faced a real storm. Read Jonah chapters 1–2. What did Jonah learn about God while he was still in the storm? What did he learn about himself?

4. Read Acts 27:13–44. Paul faced many storms in his life. How did he respond to this particular storm, even though he was a prisoner in chains? In spite of his wisdom and strength, how was Paul relying on God during this episode? Why do we sometimes forget to pray for our leaders?

5. Read Acts 28:1–10. How can you see that God was in charge? Judging from verses 14–16, who do you think were Paul's comforters besides the Lord?

6. Read Psalm 27. What is the trouble David speaks about in this psalm? In verses 4–9 David talks about the source of his strength. Which of these verses strikes you particularly and why? Which relationships does David mention in verses 10–12, and what state were they in?

How Should I Pray?

- Pray for Christians in the storm of persecution.
- Pray for people weathering the storm of poverty.
- Pray for people coping with the storm of physical or mental handicaps.
- Pray for people battling the storms of addiction, imprisonment, abandonment and rejection because of bad choices.

- Pray for leaders in the church, government, schools and missions.

- We bring some storms on ourselves. Pray for people you know who have done that.

- Pray Jonah's prayer in Jonah 2.

- Pray Psalm 27:13–14 for yourself, your family and others in need.

CHAPTER TWELVE

PLANNING TO BE PART OF HIS PLAN

No plan of yours can be thwarted.

JOB 42:2

Do not conform any longer to the pattern of this world but be transformed by the renewing of your mind. Then you will be able to test and approve what God's will is—his good, pleasing and perfect will.

ROMANS 12:2

JOB lived in God's world, spent time in God's waiting room and found out that it was all part of God's will. It is God's will that we live in the right way in a world gone wrong, and we can't do that unless we understand a little of God's plan. Job talked about the plan of God. He believed with all of his heart that there was one.

When trouble comes to you, it can often seem as if confusion reigns, and there are no orderly workings anywhere in the whole universe. And yet Job insisted there was a plan. When someone messes up your plans, it's a great joy to believe no one can mess up God's plan for you!

What do we mean by "God's plan"? It's the same as His will—what He wants to happen. It's what He has in mind. The apostle Paul told us that God's will is "good, and acceptable, and perfect" (Rom. 12:2, KJV), but therein lies the trouble. How can you possibly believe you are in God's will and that it is good when you are nursing a terminally ill patient, standing in horror in the killing fields of Cambodia or reading about the genocide in Rwanda? What's good, perfect or acceptable about any of that? What's good, perfect and acceptable about a marriage that ends, a child who goes off the rails or a church that splits?

The only logical conclusion you can come to is that we must be talking about something else when we talk about the good, perfect and acceptable will of God. Again, in Philip Yancey's words, we mustn't "confuse life with God."

GOD'S PLANS

First of all, we need to believe that God is an orderly God, that He does have a purpose and that His purpose hasn't changed. He is a purposeful God. He is not haphazard or random. His universe works like heavenly clockwork. There are laws of nature in the universe that the life of other worlds depends on, and the Bible claims that God wrote, implements and controls those laws. In the same way, the laws of human behavior that God has ordained will bring order to the chaos of our relationships if we let Him control us. He has a purpose and plan for the creatures of His universe as surely as He has a plan for that universe.

Second, God has the power to maintain the created order of things that submit to His control. He is omniscient and omnipotent; "all things were created by Him and for Him" (Col. 1:16). There is an overarching purpose for it all: that all of creation bring glory to the Creator, and rightly so. When we order our lives according to the God of order, good and glory are the results.

Third, it is God's plan that everything out of control be brought into subjection to Him to honor and praise His name. What then does He have in mind for the wicked and for this world gone mad? A plan of renewal, regeneration and redemption. This plan includes that creatures having a free will—namely, human beings like us—willingly accept His way to that renewal or reject it. One way or another God's plan is, in the end, a new heaven and a new earth (Rev. 21:1), where righteousness dwells and where all who plan to be part of His plan will live together in harmony. To this end, all things are working together for that ultimate good (Rom. 8:28).

The Opposing Plan

But Satan has a plan too. It is not a plan of order but rather of chaos. The devil is the author of confusion. He tries to thwart the plan of God, that is, the big plan—the plan of redemption.

The Bible has plenty to tell us about Satan. Second Corinthians 2:11 says that we are not (meaning that we shouldn't be) "unaware of his schemes"; in 4:4 it says plainly that Satan blinds the minds of those who don't believe in Jesus. He plans our eternal destruction and tempts us by all means to that end. There is a battle going on for the minds of us human beings. As someone noted, "The wholeness of our hurt can be felt in the attacks of Satan—sometimes against our body, often against our minds, usually against our pride, and always against our faith."[1]

It's really fairly simple. Satan sees the potential for evil in every human being, and he exploits it as much as he can. If we give him a little foothold, he will use it for all it's worth. A little jealousy? He will energize it until it becomes deep, hateful resentment. A little self-centeredness? He can blow it into egomania in one conversation. Haven't you ever left a situation, asking yourself how things got so out of control? Haven't we all been in conflicts that started as simple misunderstandings and ended up as deeply fractured relationships, almost beyond mending? This is Satan's specialty—to take not only our sinful tendencies but also our honest mistakes and weaknesses, and create out of them the biggest, most painful situations he can.

If the devil does all of this with human nature, it only follows that he uses suffering to his own end also. Suffering opens to Satan the chance to exploit the depravity of the human heart. This is why, in the middle of a crisis, there is usually someone making matters worse—looters after a fire, price gouging of badly needed items after a flood or hurricane—when people are already devastated. Satan is the source of a teenager's parents being told it is their fault their child committed suicide or got into trouble. Whatever can be heaped on painful fires to keep them burning, our Enemy is always willing to supply. All he needs are people who have not committed themselves to God's plan, to His purposes and to being filled with God's nature.

We have no real idea what, if anything, God had explained to Job about Satan and his schemes—about his origins, his fall, and his diabolical intentions. Yet Job comes out with another classic statement of fact and faith. "I know that you can do all things; no plan of yours can be thwarted" (Job 42:2).

The big plan in heaven is for God to gather out a people for Himself from every tongue, tribe and nation (Rev. 5:9)—a people who will be obedient and reflect His image and glory, a people He will gift with eternal life. He is "not willing that any should perish, but that all should come to repentance" (2 Pet. 3:9, KJV). It is God's will that all of us should come to receive these eternal gifts, but it is His knowledge of the future that tells Him all will not choose to come. However, His stated will and purpose promise that those who come will have eternal life in another dimension with Him. That's an incredible plan!

What's more, God is clever enough and strong enough to do it! If Genesis had already been written, Job would have loved reading chapter 18, where an angel tells Abraham, an old man in his nineties, that he is going to have a baby with his elderly wife, Sarah. When Sarah goes into mild hysterics at this piece of startling information, the Lord says to Abraham, "Why did Sarah laugh? . . . Is anything too hard for the LORD?" (Gen. 18:13–14). Now there's the challenge. Can the plan of God be thwarted? No! If He is the author of life, then He can bring life out of deadness (Heb. 11:12). Nothing is too hard for Him, and soon, young Isaac was running around to prove it! Do you believe God can bring life out of a dead heart, a dead marriage, a dead situation?

God is working His purposes out, and even though Satan tries to thwart those purposes, it's a lost cause. Jesus—God in human form—put the devil in his place at Calvary. Satan is a defeated foe, trying to do as much damage as he can because he knows that "his time is short" (Rev. 12:12).

So God's plan is the redemption of the world. He has even told us how this plan of His will work and how people will find out about it.

SEEING GOD'S PLAN IN CREATION

When I was fourteen years of age, my father took the family to the continent of Europe for a holiday. One evening we found ourselves in the breathtakingly beautiful Swiss Alps. This was in the years after World War II, and everyone was taking advantage of traveling. For this reason all the bed-and-breakfasts were full. "There is nothing else for it," my father said, "but to spend the night in the car; it's too dangerous to drive on, on these treacherous mountain roads." So my parents, my sister and I settled down in a medium-sized car to try to get some sleep.

I found myself wide-awake in the early morning hours, fidgeting around, trying to get comfortable. In the end I abandoned the task and left the vehicle near the rest area where we had parked, wandered up to the mountain road, found a rock and sat there, watching the sunrise.

Unchurched, ignorant of the gospel, without Christ, without God and without hope, I found myself caught up in the incredible regeneration of a brand-new day. Something began to stir my fourteen-year-old heart. It was breathtaking. It was as if the angels stretched the dawn tightly over a canvas and held it firmly in place while the Lord dipped His brush in heaven's paint box and painted me a picture of Himself. I was mesmerized—overcome with awe—and I was convicted. For the first time in my young life, I was aware of God's brightness—and how tarnished my own soul was.

I went back to the car to find my sketch pad, returned and, instead of having the audacity to attempt catching God's colors on my little pad of paper made out of His trees, wrote my first piece of poetry:

> The dawn breaks softly
> filling me with awe.
> It seems the other side of heaven's door.
> That God forgives men's sins to me is plain;
> today in spite of my sin,
> the sun did rise again!

I was on the way home! Creation had spoken to a teenager, sitting on a rock in the Swiss Alps, on a continental holiday with her family, and I was never to be the same again!

God has written His plan in His creation so that every man, woman and child will have a chance to "read" creation and understand what God is really like. Job 38–42 reveals how much Job came to understand about God through creation. Romans tells us, "Since earliest times men have seen the earth and sky and all God made, and have known of his existence and great eternal power. So they will have no excuse" (Rom. 1:20, TLB).

One day, when people stand before God, they will not be able to say they knew nothing about Him. There is enough to explain His eternal power and divine nature in the things He has made that should lead them to reach out and seek Him. I know this from my own experience.

There is no question in my mind that God does not live in a church-shaped box. He is omnipresent and especially visible in the things He has made. I had seen enough already, without any further explanation, to believe that God was a powerful, creative being and also full of grace. In spite of the sin He had just revealed, I looked at the reflection of who He was and believed. He had revisited my little world, giving me another day and another chance to come near enough to be forgiven and stay close enough to be strengthened!

I am convinced that God spoke to Job and his four friends, in the days before other means were available, through His incredible creative genius, in the same way He spoke to me. Eliphaz said, "He performs wonders that cannot be fathomed, miracles that cannot be counted" (Job 5:9). He asked, "Is not God in the heights of heaven? And see how lofty are the highest stars! Yet you say, 'What does God know? Does he judge through such darkness? Thick clouds veil him, so he does not see us as he goes about in the vaulted heavens'" (22:12–14).

Bildad said, "Dominion and awe belong to God; he establishes order in the heights of heaven. . . . If even the moon is not bright and the stars are not pure in his eyes, how much less man, who is but a maggot—a son of man, who is only a worm!" (25:2, 5–6). Zophar testifies, "The heavens will expose [the sinner's] guilt; the earth will rise up against him" (20:27). That is my testimony too.

Do you know people who lull themselves into a false sense of security because they have avoided exposing themselves to Christians, church or the gospel? The Bible says there is enough of God to be seen to convict and convince people of His power, majesty and holiness—and their own sin—so that they are "without excuse."

Seeing God's Plan in God's People

God's plan is also evident in the lives of His children. Job bore witness to the God of creation he had come to know, and he spoke rightly about that God of grace, who was coming to save him. He knew all about the big plan, the plan that was bigger than his little plans for peace and prosperity. Thus he could proclaim to the world, "I know that my Redeemer lives!" I too can testify that I saw God not only in His creation but also in one of His children—a creature of His creative genius. It was through someone who knew Him, who shared His plan of salvation with me, even as Job shared it with his friends, that I found myself planning to be part of God's plan.

I was in the hospital, and the girl in the next bed explained further what I already knew in essence. She showed me how to come close enough to be forgiven. She asked me if I knew I was a sinner who needed a Savior. When I said yes, she explained how, at Bethlehem, this great Creator God had become one of the creatures He had made. "Why did He come?" I asked, although I already knew the facts. "Christ came to be the Savior of a world gone wrong," she explained. I needed to take a personal approach to the general truth and to make Him my Redeemer as men and women have done all through history. She helped me understand what she was talking about, and she led me to the cross in prayer. Then, almost in Job's words, I was able to say, "My ears had heard of you, but now my eyes have seen you." I was home. Having begun to search for Him in my teenage years, through the witness of creation, I now understood how I could find Him, helped to commitment through one of His own.

Now I was part of the big plan, God's plan for the world. I knew it and I was excited! Christ had redeemed me to be part of His ongoing purpose. He had reconciled me to Himself through the death of His Son and had given me the ministry of reconciliation (2 Cor. 5:18).

To be part of such a plan blew my mind! I felt a huge sense of value, of worth. I had become part of a plan that would, from that time forward, see me over my head in involvement with street kids, families, counseling, preaching and teaching the word of reconciliation literally around the world. What a privilege and what adventure—enough for a lifetime. To know that my earthly assignment was a plan of God that could not be thwarted made my future shine as brightly as that first sunrise I witnessed in the Swiss Alps!

One right thing Eliphaz said was that the Lord "thwarts the plans of the crafty" (Job 5:12). Satan was my enemy, but God was now my friend who would be my advocate in heaven and would pray for me as I got involved with His mission in bringing His plan to others.

What is God's plan? In a nutshell it is that we should go into all the world and preach this good, redemptive story, especially to the wicked—sinners—the people who, like Job and his friends, and like me and my friends, only needed the explanation of the gospel to grasp it with both hands. I realized then that most of the world had not rejected the gospel; they simply hadn't had a chance to hear and accept it. Not long ago, I was in Taiwan and saw the wonder of this yet again.

Cooperating with God

Stuart and I had been invited to conduct some leadership meetings with missionaries in Asia. During our stay we visited some of the places where these missionaries and nationals were working. I was asked to go with a woman evangelist, Bea Chan, into a Taiwan prison and speak to young delinquents, many of them murderers.

On the car journey to one venue, I asked Bea to tell me her story. How did she come to Christ and get so fully involved in her ministry of reconciliation? "In God's plan," she began, and my mind flew to Job and stayed there as she described her terrible childhood.

She was only four years of age when her desperate mother put her and her two-year-old sister in the arms of a twelve-year-old aunt, got them passage on a boat leaving Communist China and sent them to Taiwan. The children found an old schoolhouse in the slums. It was decrepit and unsafe, but they set themselves to survive. The aunt found some work she could do for a missionary, and Bea was left to care for her little sister. That was hard, responsible work for such a young child.

The aunt heard about God and the gospel from the missionary she worked for and felt obliged to take her nieces along to Sunday school. Bea listened intently and wondered if it was true that God cared about them. Surely if there was such a great God in heaven like the one she was hearing about, then He was too big and too busy to care about them. She wondered if there was any way she could find out.

One day her three-year-old sister would not stop crying. Bea tried in vain to comfort her and decided to take her outside their old, rickety schoolhouse to try to distract her attention. As soon as she stepped outside the house, the roof collapsed! "That's when I believed that God cared about little things like me and my sister and that He had protected us," she told me.

As she grew up, she came to believe that God had a plan for her life. It was simply to cooperate with her Redeemer and tell others about Him. Like Job, she never focused on the whys.

She didn't ask, "Why did my mother send me away? Why am I so far from home? Why do we live in poverty? Why is there no medicine when we get sick?" Instead, she thought of God's provision and protection for them in their trouble, thanking Him for saving their lives and saving their souls. She determined from childhood that she would become one of Job's daughters.

That day in the prison she said to me, "We have one hour with these young people. Just remember, probably not one of them has heard the name of Jesus once!"

"What do I say to them?" I asked her.

"Tell them about the plan," she said. "Tell them the gospel, but start with Genesis." And so I told them the story and that no plan of God's can be thwarted. "He has a plan for each of you, too, and it is a wonderful, wonderful plan," I said.

What incredible joy to watch Bea first interpret my words, then explain how they could know this Creator God, who had been brought within reach of the worst sinner by Christ their Savior. She explained how they could receive the Holy Spirit. Boy after boy raised his hand or stood to his feet to ask for help to pray to this loving God. They came close enough to be forgiven and, we hope, have since stayed near enough to be strengthened! I wondered, as I left the prison that day, how many would become a "Job" for their friends—and their enemies—and for whatever remnant of a family they would return to when they got out of jail. I pray for them as I pray for my own family, that they will desire to be part of God's plan.

What Does It Mean?

1. Imagine you are in a living room with people who have never heard that God has a plan. Describe what God's plan is without using Scripture or religious jargon. Give

an example of how the plan of God has been proved to be good, perfect and acceptable in your own life.

2. Discuss or write about Philip Yancey's premise: "We mustn't confuse life with God."

3. Discuss or write about Satan's plan. How do we know it will fail?

4. Share or write about an experience of how someone has helped you to accept, understand or fulfill God's plan.

5. Read Romans 1. Make a list of all the things this chapter teaches us about the plan of God.

6. Read Romans 12:1–2. What conditions must be fulfilled before the will of God, whatever it is, can become acceptable to us?

7. If God allows Satan to tempt us when trouble comes, what do these words of Job mean: "No plan of yours can be thwarted" (Job 42:2)? Discuss or write a paragraph about this.

8. Think of an important decision you need to make. Perhaps it's hard to make a choice between two good things. Make a list of pros and cons. Ask God to help you "prove" what His plan is.

How Should I Pray?

- Pray about the lists you made for number 8 above. Sometimes it is easier to say God's will is good and perfect than to say it's acceptable. What helped Job to submit and accept what had happened to him?

- Pray for people you love to accept the will of God for their lives.

- Pray for people who have gotten off track to be restored.

- Pray for God's "big plan" to be completed.

- Pray for people who are close to you—that they will get around to planning to be part of God's plan.

CHAPTER THIRTEEN

FINDING THE HEART TO FORGIVE

My servant Job will pray for you, and I will accept his prayer.

JOB 42:8

And when you stand praying, if you hold anything against anyone,
forgive him, so that your Father in heaven may forgive you your sins.

MARK 11:25

LEWIS Smedes writes that "irritability is the launching pad for anger." If irritability isn't checked, it will soon flare into hostility. We will see the person we are angry with as the foe. There is enough selfishness in all of us to keep the quarrel going. We don't naturally want to make peace; in fact, we are far too ready to grab our gun and declare war. Anger is like the blast of a bullet. It is violence spewing out of a hurt heart, intent on doing as much damage as possible.

Some anger is undoubtedly legitimate. There is such a thing as holy wrath. "After the LORD had said these things to Job, he said to Eliphaz the Temanite, 'I am angry with you and your two friends'" (Job 42:7). We know that God's anger is a wholly legitimate anger.

God even tells us why He is angry. He is angry with the three friends because they haven't spoken rightly about Him. They have misrepresented Him. They have purported to say how He behaves—that He, by deliberately sending suffering, punishes the sinner who has already been justified. This throws God into a bad light. It makes of Him a vengeful being who is lacking in mercy and compassion. Those men have twisted God's revelation of Himself, and that is why He is angry with them.

This makes me not a little nervous. I teach the Bible. I do my best to study and learn it first. I try to correctly handle the word of truth (2 Tim. 2:15). I realize how extremely important it is to teach the whole counsel of God and not become unbalanced. Job's friends majored on the justice of God at the expense of the mercy of God, and it led them to draw a caricature of His character. No wonder God was not pleased!

Those of us who teach the Scriptures need to be sure we are speaking correctly about God to others, or we run the risk of God's anger. That thought should keep us on track if nothing else does! So there is an anger that is legitimate.

It's right to be angry about theological error, and it's right to be angry about human error too, especially when it affects other people. Job says, "Have I not wept for those in trouble? Has not my soul grieved for the poor?" (Job 30:25). God is shown throughout the Old Testament and much of the New Testament as being angry when the innocent, the poor and the underprivileged are bullied or victimized. He is angry with the people of Israel when they don't look after prisoners properly or care for the widows, the orphans and the stranger within their gates. If He is angry about that, we should be too. Good anger about the circumstances of those less fortunate than we are can motivate us to serve them.

Over and over again God calls Job "my servant." At the beginning of the book, He asks Satan twice, "Have you considered my servant Job?" At the end of the book He rebukes Job's friends and again uses the phrase, "You have not spoken of me what is right, as my servant Job has." And finally, "My servant Job will pray for you" (42:7–8).

God knows that part of being a servant is being angry: angry at man's inhumanity to man; mad at people whose selfishness and tyranny, conflicts and terrorism, cause pain and heartache; angry at people who could alleviate suffering and don't.

I have lots of chances to be angry because, as I travel and meet people in many locations and situations, I see a lot of cruel things happening to the innocent. Not too long ago I was speaking at a rescue mission fund-raiser in a large city. I arrived in the afternoon and was given a tour of the nice, modern buildings. As the director was showing me around, there was a commotion in the reception area. A mother and her children were crying in the lobby, and helpers were carrying in furniture, clothes, some bedding, pans and groceries. They had just been evicted from a house down the street. They had not been able to pay their rent because the father of the family, a white man, had AIDS and had returned to his parents' home to die, leaving his wife, a black woman, and her children to their fate. His family, who had never approved of the marriage, refused to help, and the inevitable result was scattered all over the lobby of the rescue mission.

The little girl was crying, "They put my bed on the street—will someone bring it in here—they put my little bed on the sidewalk—please, someone!" Praise God for His servants in that place. The rescue mission staff was angry at the callous way these particular authorities had dealt so abruptly with the family. They were also rightly angry with the thieves who had run off with the six-year-old's bed before they could walk the couple of blocks and rescue it from the sidewalk. They told the little girl she was right to be angry about it, because they were, and they believed God was too. At this point I felt that they reflected exactly what God must have been feeling about the whole situation.

One reason God is angry with Job's friends is that they are apparently willing to debate only theology and not to be practically involved in serving Job's obvious needs. Jesus addresses this in Matthew 25: "For I was hungry and you wouldn't feed me; thirsty, and you wouldn't give me anything to drink; a stranger, and you refused me hospitality; naked, and you wouldn't clothe me; sick, and in prison, and you didn't visit me" (25:42–43, TLB).

When we see Job sitting on his ash heap covered with boils, we need to try to get him some medicine. When it's lunchtime, someone needs to buy him some food to give him strength. Someone else needs to keep him supplied with lots of fluids and find some clean clothes for him to wear. And yet another needs to find him a bed to sleep in. We must help in tangible, practical ways. When we do, Jesus says He sees our efforts, and it's just as if we were doing it for Him. If we don't use our God-given resources to alleviate the suffering of others, it's just as if we are neglecting Him! He takes this personally and very seriously indeed, and so should we. So there is a good anger—a righteous indignation.

When do we have a right to be angry with people for the way they have treated us? We can be angry at the same injustice and cruelty that would make us angry for the sake of someone else. God is angry when others mistreat us, when our needs are ignored, when people are insensitive and selfish, and we suffer as a result. We don't gain anything by denying that something is wrong, that we've been hurt. But we also don't gain anything by staying angry. Many of us get stuck in our anger. When anger turns into bottled-up resentment, Satan uses our hurt to create something even more evil. It is at this point that we may sin. If anger is not dealt with, it can be a form of slow suicide, destroying the insides of our stomach and our soul.

Angry at God

Some people are angry at God. They are mad because He didn't intervene, that He allowed Satan through the hedge and did nothing about it. They want to pay someone back for what has happened to them, but they don't know how to pay God back. So they cold-shoulder Him, curse Him, keep their distance. In fact, as David Augsburger says in his book *The Freedom of Forgiveness*, "I can hate him. I can nurse a grudge until it grows into a full-grown hate—hooves, horns, tail and all."[1]

Satan loves it when we are mad at God. It is then that we are most like Satan! He also knows that resentment cuts us off from the only source of help we have. If he can get us to turn our backs on God, we can't see God's face and see that there are tears in His eyes.

Although Job has never been guilty of some of the things his friends accuse him of, in his extremity he does become resentful toward God. He's a long way off from cursing God, but he is accusing God of unfair treatment. Elihu points this out to Job. He says to him, "But you have said in my hearing . . . [God] considers me his enemy" (Job 33:8, 10). Job is at the lowest of his lowest points. He says, "I am pure and without sin; I am clean and free from guilt. Yet God has found fault with me; he considers me his enemy. He fastens my feet in shackles" (33:9–10). Job is saying that God has treated him like a prisoner and not a friend.

Have you ever felt that God has treated you unfairly? That you're just a chess piece being moved around between God and Satan? One college student reflected, "During some of my worst times, I've felt that life is just a big game God is playing—that what I want or need doesn't even matter. But that theory falls apart when I consider that Jesus Christ came to earth, lived and was tortured to death. Would God have done this for the sake of a game? I don't understand why God is silent sometimes or why He prevents some things and allows others. But our lives are not trivial to Him—not as long as there is a Savior and a cross. That was God suffering—for our sakes. Not a game at all."

Elihu reminds Job that a man needs to ask God to forgive him for thinking God to be unfair. He also reminds Job that he can establish a closer relationship with God than he ever had before, find a new experience of joy and renewal, forgiveness and grace, and become an enthusiastic witness for the Lord (33:26–28).

When we get around to telling God we are sorry, sorry for our suspicions that He has been using us or playing with us; when we ask God to forgive us for all our perceived notions, then we will be restored to the source of power we are going to need if we are to forgive everyone else. Looking back, we will then be able to see that He was there all the time. We will even see His footprints in the sands of our suffering.

> He led me by a way of pain
> A barren and a starless place;
> (I did not know His eyes were wet
> He would not let me see His face.)
> He left me like a frightened child
> Unshielded in the night of storm,
> (How should I dream He was so near?
> The rainswept darkness hid His form.)
> But when the clouds were drifting back
> And dawn was breaking into day,
> I knew whose feet had walked with mine;
> I saw His footprints all the way.
> —Anonymous

I can only remember once being angry at God for His apparent neglect. It was the most miserable experience, and not until I told Him how sorry I was and reaffirmed my belief in His character and care was I in the position to truly pray about the situation. Job asks God to forgive him for his attitude and wrong thinking. "I loathe myself," he says (42:6, TLB). Like Isaiah, he laments, "Woe to me." Job decides that whatever God decides is going to be all right with him. What God does or doesn't do is right. His plan is perfect. At this point God helps Job begin to see himself not as victim but as victor!

Author and biblical scholar Gleason Archer says, "The right use of suffering leads to a complete and unreserved surrender to the will of God without rebellion or willfulness of any kind. It prepares a man for complete restoration and a new life of peace and joy and fellowship with God." This is what Elihu is promising Job. You will find the effect in your body, he says: "Then his flesh is renewed like a child's; it is restored as in the days of his youth" (33:25). You will find the results of spiritual renewal in your soul, he assures Job: "He prays to God and finds favor with him, he sees God's face and shouts for joy; he is restored by God to his righteous state" (33:26). Soon he will be restored to his ministry too.

There's hardly any need to mention what scientists and doctors have discovered about the effects of anger and anxiety on our bodies, minds and emotions. Elihu knew, long before medical science, that a soul cleansed by forgiveness and reconciliation makes for health in the entire person.

Then the person who has been wounded, who is now restored to relationship with God, can say to others, "I sinned, and perverted what was right, but I did not get what I deserved. He redeemed my soul from going down to the pit, and I will live to enjoy the light" (33:27–28).

This reminds me of David's psalm of restoration—Psalm 51. David has been justified. He was a man after God's own heart, but he has sinned with Bathsheba. His neighbor was out of town on business, and he took his wife and committed adultery with her. After David's repentance, God restored him. "Restore to me the joy of your salvation and grant me a willing spirit, to sustain me. Then I will teach transgressors your ways, and sinners will turn back to you," David prayed (51:12–13). The effect of his spiritual renaissance was blessing for others. It happened this way for David and the people around him—and it is the same with Job. When we have sorted things out for ourselves, others in turn can experience blessing.

The Way of Reconciliation

God tells Job's three friends that they need to say they are sorry to Job. They are to take seven bulls and seven rams and go to God's "servant" and sacrifice a burnt offering for themselves. "My servant Job will pray for you, and I will accept his prayer and not deal with you according to your folly." God says, in effect, "I will forgive you, and Job will forgive you! He is now in a position to be able to do that." After the friends had done what God told them to do, Job prayed for them, and God accepted his prayer (Job 42:9).

Years ago, I was an angry young woman. Stuart and I served a youth organization that I felt demanded unreasonable amounts of our time. The angrier I got, the worse I felt. I would go to bed angry and get up angry. I didn't like the way God and the mission were doing things. Needless to say, I neglected my Bible, prayer and church. One day I found myself sick of being sick of it! I was tired of the frustration that was spilling over into my family. I began shouting at the kids. A friend was over and noticed how bad-tempered I was. I blamed the children. "They're driving me crazy!" I said. Quietly my friend (and she was a true friend to confront me) said, "Children don't create your attitude, Jill; they reveal it!" Ouch! It was true. A cup filled with sweet water cannot spill one bitter drop! When my "cup" was jogged, what was in it came out—bitterness, anger, frustration and hurt. Whoever was nearest me got wet!

In the end I went to one of Job's daughters. I took my seven bulls and seven rams and arrived at her door with enough evidence of my chagrin to convince her I meant business. She, a true servant of the living God, accepted my offering and prayed for me, even though much of my anger was directed toward her. I can't tell you how humbled, yet how happy, I was after that.

Chapter 42 is full of happy people. I believe even Eliphaz, Bildad and Zophar, and certainly Elihu, felt the restoration of God in their own hearts as surely as Job felt it in his. What a load of garbage we get rid of when we say we are sorry, first and foremost when we say it to God and then when we say it to whomever else we need to say it to.

Job forgave God, and then he forgave his friends. Whom do you need to forgive? Let me encourage you to do that, as Elihu encouraged Job. After you do, God will restore you, and you will "see God's face and shout for joy." Notice it was after Job prayed for his friends that the Lord restored him. "After Job had prayed for his friends, the LORD made him prosperous again and gave him twice as much as he had before" (42:10). There are conditions to forgiveness on a human level. God is in the reconciliation business and expects us to be in it too, but we need to make sure we have fulfilled the conditions first. I'm pretty sure Job had already sacrificed his own bulls and rams before his friends appeared with theirs. He had to understand the size of his own forgiveness all over again before he could forgive other people's little sins. When we realize the huge heap of our own transgressions and what a burden our own personal iniquity is for our Redeemer, other people's little backpacks of naughtiness seem small enough for us to manage.

MENDING ONLY GOD CAN DO

The story is told of an African man who had a dream. He was toiling up a hill. At the crest were three crosses, and he realized he was at Calvary. Suddenly he became aware of another figure walking up the hill toward the cross, a figure he recognized as the Lord Jesus Christ. The bowed form had a huge bundle on his back so that it was nearly broken. From his brow ran beads of sweat, which looked like blood.

"Master!" the African man cried out. "Are you carrying the sins of the whole world to Calvary?"

"No," said Christ, "only yours!"

When we realize how much we have been forgiven, we will be in a better frame of mind when Eliphaz, Bildad and Zophar appear and ask us to forgive them.

So Job forgave his friends, and also his family. He had lamented in Job 16:7, "Surely, O God, you have worn me out; you have devastated my entire household." Remember, Job's family structure was a little different from ours! The extended family had become estranged from Job, adding sorrow upon sorrow. "My kinsmen have gone away. . . . I am loathsome to my own brothers," he laments.

Yet now we see that "all his brothers and sisters and everyone who had known him before came and ate with him in his house. They comforted and consoled him over all the trouble the LORD had brought upon him, and each one gave him a piece of silver and a gold ring" (42:11). Even Job's wife must have reconciled with him, although some commentaries speculate that he may have taken a new wife. Anyway, they had seven more sons and three daughters, so they must have made up!

"Well," you might be saying, "everyone probably came around because the Lord made him prosperous again." Not necessarily. God used them to make Job prosperous—"each one gave him a piece of silver and a gold ring." Now Job could restock his cattle sheds. So they must have reconciled before God blessed him again.

Why then did they gather around when they had rejected him before? There is only one good explanation for that: the Lord blessed him. The Lord made him prosperous—not only in riches but with the richness of restored relationships, a gift that is impossible to purchase!

Only God can mend some marriages. Only God can bring brother and brother, sister and father, son and mother together again. He is the author of unity and harmony. It is Satan who is the author of confusion and division. But there is a principle here. If you are sitting on the ash heap of all of your relationships, know that revival starts with you. Who knows what God will do in the future in our relationships? Only He knows. But we can say, "Whatever others do about the divisions in this family, I will do my part." After all, we are only responsible for our own actions and attitudes and not for anyone else's.

I believe God gave Job the ability to forgive everybody who needed forgiving. He knew there is a prosperity of spirit that can only be enjoyed when friends and family and even enemies are offered forgiveness. Jesus said we are to love our enemies and bless those who persecute us (Matt. 5:43–44).

The Power of Forgiveness

I have had the privilege of meeting a Job or two who demonstrate such a prosperity of spirit by loving their enemies that they truly reflect the image of God.

I met such a man in Croatia. I think of him as a modern-day Job and his wife and daughter as Job's daughters. He is a pastor in the little Croatian town of Pak Rak. The town was blasted to pieces during the war with Serbia, and only three houses in the main street were left standing. The little church where Bozidar Korlovic was pastor was severely damaged, and even though the uneasy ceasefire was broken between the warring factions, the pastor and his seventeen-year-old daughter returned. They wanted to encourage others to come back and pick up the bits of their shattered lives. The little town was surrounded by Serb-occupied Croatian territory, and the Serb soldiers were visible in the hills around.

One day when the pastor and his daughter were walking to their house, Serb soldiers came through the trees and took them prisoner. They marched them up the hill to the tree line and tortured him and took his daughter off with them. After they thrust Bozidar through seven times with a bayonet, he was still alive. "You can kill our bodies, but you cannot kill our souls!" he told them. "God will bring you to judgment for these cruel things, but if you repent, He will forgive you." In the end they sent the two home through a minefield! God kept them safe, and the United Nations forces rescued them.

I stood in his little church a brief fourteen months later as he talked about that terrible time. We listened as Bozidar and his wife testified to a church packed with refugees. They told them that they had forgiven the Serbs for all of it. "We must forgive our enemies," he told them with passion. "The Lord will help us. Only is love is sufficient." I thought of Job. I know he forgave the Sabeans and the Chaldeans for putting all his servants, many of whom would have been born in his household, to the sword. If they had tortured Job himself, he would have forgiven them for that as well. No wonder God prospered Job. The prosperity of spirit that makes the soul fat has little to do with monetary wealth.

Whom do you need to forgive? Your friends, family, servants, the Chaldeans or Sabeans? What do you need to forgive? The only place it's possible is at the foot of the cross. There the death of Christ gives us power and permission to leave the judgment of the issues involved to Him and to reconcile!

What Does It Mean?

1. What is the difference between holy wrath and unholy wrath? Does it surprise you to read that God was angry with Job's "miserable comforters"? Why or why not?

2. Does prayer help you forgive someone? Does it alter your attitude toward people? Give examples.

3. Read Job 32:1–12. Why was Elihu the last to speak to Job? Do you ever feel you are too young, too inexperienced, or too lacking in biblical knowledge to contribute an opinion? What most hinders you from making a contribution? What do we learn from Elihu's example?

4. Read First Timothy 4:12–16. How were Elihu and Timothy alike? How can Paul's words to Timothy encourage us?

5. Read Psalm 51. Why do you suppose verses 1–12 precede verses 13–15? Read Job 42:5–6, Psalm 51:17 and Isaiah 6:5. What do all these verses have in common?

6. Look up the following verses; choose one to memorize:
   • Psalm 34:18
   • Psalm 51:17
   • 2 Corinthians 7:10

7. The picture we are left with in Job 42 is one of reconciliation. This is what God wants. Read Jesus' prayer in John 17:22–26. Write in your own words what Jesus was praying for us.

8. Read the Lord's Prayer in Matthew 6:9–13. What does it teach you about reconciliation?

How Should I Pray?

Pray that:

- God would show you the things you should be angry about
- God would help you deal with the things you shouldn't be angry about
- you will be a Timothy or an Elihu to someone who needs you badly.

Pray for:

- a sense of God's holiness and your own unworthiness
- people in your family with whom you need to reconcile
- people in your family who need to reconcile with each other.

Pray the Lord's Prayer.

CHAPTER FOURTEEN

JOB'S DAUGHTERS

The first daughter he named Jemimah, the second Keziah and the third Keren-Happuch. Nowhere in all the land were there found women as beautiful as Job's daughters, and their father granted them an inheritance along with their brothers.

JOB 42:14–15

She is clothed with strength and dignity; she can laugh at the days to come.

PROVERBS 31:25

SINCE Stuart and I were in Brazil with the Wycliffe Bible Translators as I was finishing this manuscript, I thought I would ask some veteran translators if they could tell me anything about the names of Job's daughters. It seemed significant to me that their names were mentioned and not the names of Job's sons. As I gleaned the information, it struck me that as Job began to experience chapter 42, he must have wanted to mark his thankfulness by giving meaningful names to his girls.

This is certainly the tradition in other cultures. I think of being introduced to a young man in Africa whose name was "Graduation" because he was born the day his father graduated from college! When I met "Bicycle" (who had been born the day his father inherited a bike from his boss), I understood that important events could be marked by bestowing significant names on one's offspring.

Job was at last coming out of the storm, and we can take heart that there will be an emerging from the storm for each one of us. The picture of a healed and helped Job prospering and being a father again is encouraging! It might well be that that experience will have to wait till we are safely home in heaven and the true chapter 42 begins. Or it may be that in God's grace, He will give us a second chance to enjoy earth's blessings "inside the hedge" down here before we enjoy it inside the glassy walls up there!

I like to think of Job's family life as this new era began, especially imagining his relationship with his girls. Isn't it true that a father and his daughter(s) often have a very special relationship? Job's suffering enabled him to give a rich inheritance to those he loved. Perhaps all of this made Satan sorry he had started the whole thing in the first place!

So what inheritance did Job give to his daughters? A godly one. A great one. A generous one. Here in chapter 42 we are reading a historical account of landholdings, cattle, camels and sheep. But Job gave his beautiful daughters far more than the wonderful things money can buy. The blessings of a regenerate family are eternal blessings that can make our lives richer than our wildest dreams.

If Job prayed so regularly and diligently for his children before his brush with death, you can be sure he prayed no less after his deepening experience with the Lord. That was one of the things he gave them. My husband was prayed for before he was born, as was his brother, Bernard. Mary and Stanley Briscoe would pray over the empty crib, asking God, as Job asked for his children, that they would always serve and honor the Lord. It is no surprise to me to see both these men serving God today all over the world. Whatever else you leave your children, leave them the legacy of prayer.

What else did Job give his daughters? He gave them an inheritance along with their brothers. The headship of man had degenerated soon after the Fall into the domination of women. It didn't take long for men to treat their women as property or slaves. But Job respected women, and as a leader, he modeled that respect.

I thank God for my own husband in this regard. Holding himself responsible as the head of our home, he has used his headship to make sure the women in his life, who are his God-given responsibility, are regarded and treated as equals. A man of quality is not threatened by a woman of equality. He is not threatened by a woman's gifts. Both our daughter, Judy, and I have benefited from Stuart's high view of women as he has counted us equal in the sight of God. He has insisted we become all the Lord has gifted us to be, and we have happily flourished in that atmosphere. Little girls, alongside little boys, need to be challenged to be all they can be for Jesus. Job modeled this for us.

The Beauty of Faith

The Bible says Job's daughters were beautiful. In fact, "nowhere in all the land were there found women as beautiful as Job's daughters" (42:15). I think there is more to that statement than meets the eye! I imagine part of their beauty was a spiritual beauty that comes from a pure heart, soul, mind and body. "A woman who fears the LORD is to be praised," says the writer of Proverbs 31 as he describes the ideal woman of faith in that chapter.

Faith is beautiful! A godly life is attractive. "Who can find a virtuous woman?" the King of Massa asks rhetorically. "She is more precious than rubies" (Prov. 31:10). In our day and age, it's tempting to think that no one is looking too hard for a virtuous woman, but there is a beauty to virtue. The serenity of a countenance that has a habit of turning Godward is a commodity taken note of in our jaded world. In other words, someone who is godly is admired and applauded, often sought after and desired. To be one of Job's daughters means to strive to be like the Lord every day of your life, to bear His image.

There was a young female Salvation Army officer assigned to a particularly difficult and dangerous area in a large industrial town. She was petite and not really an eye-catcher, but she had a sweet smile and bright eyes.

She was doing her round of the bars, selling the Army's newspaper, *The War Cry*, when she noticed she was coming to her last stop. This bar was an exceptionally difficult one—it was rowdy and bawdy and always a favorite for the riffraff of the area. As she drew near, the sounds of raucous and rude singing met her full force, and she hesitated to enter. She was young and vulnerable and new to the Army, and she was scared. However, she knew that courage was "doing without the courage," so she took a deep breath, opened the door and walked in. At first the men—and it was mostly men—ignored her, but then a really huge drunk caught sight of her and walked over, swung her up in the air, and stood her on the bar. "Sing one of your songs!" shouted a young fellow loudly. "Yes, go on," said the giant, spilling beer all over the place. "Sing us a hymn—got your tambourine?" Laughter and ribald comments spilled out of the mouths of the men and women in that dark place, and the tiny recruit felt her heart beating against her rib cage as if it were eager to escape.

She took a deep breath and said in a shaky voice, "All right, I'll do it," and she began to sing one of her favorite hymns:

> Oh, to be like Thee! blessed Redeemer,
> This is my constant longing and prayer.
> Gladly I'll forfeit all of earth's treasures,
> Jesus, Thy perfect likeness to wear.

Oh, to be like Thee! full of compassion,
Loving, forgiving, tender and kind,
Helping the helpless, cheering the fainting,
Seeking the wand'ring sinner to find.

Oh, to be like Thee! while I am pleading,
Pour out Thy Spirit, fill with Thy love;
Make me a temple meet for Thy dwelling,
Fit me for life and heaven above.

The crowd became silent, mesmerized by her face and voice—weak at first and a little shaky, but growing stronger and more confident as the song went on. The girl was transformed. Her eyes sparkled, and her cheeks were flushed with excitement. And her smile! It would have charmed a duck out of water! She was truly one of Job's daughters—she could have been called Keziah, like Job's second girl, a name that means "Cassia; a fragrant herb." She brought the breath of heaven into that bar that day, and her gentle godliness carried a fragrance of life as she brought her message in song about the love of God. The rough, tough people she had committed her life to serving listened attentively, sensing God's presence. As she came to the end she sang the chorus with all her heart:

Oh, to be like Thee! Oh, to be like Thee,
Blessed Redeemer, pure as Thou art!
Come in Thy sweetness, come in Thy fullness;
Stamp Thine own image deep on my heart.[1]

She stopped. There was an unearthly silence. Then the big giant lifted her ever so gently down to the floor, saying as he did so, "Don't worry, lass, you're like Him all right. We can all see it. You're like Him!" Oh, to help our children to see that in our narcissistic society beauty comes from deep within and springs from clean hands and a humble heart that loves the Lord. If only our daughters would grow up with their souls singing, "Oh, to be like Thee!"

The Good Life

Job had something else to give to his daughters. He had the means to enable them to live life to the fullest. The picture we have at the end of the story is one of prosperity and contentment, of a lively life with the best that a world of privilege and peace can bring. That was all part of their inheritance.

We who are so privileged to live in the Western world can give our children such a heritage, and if we can, we should: the blessings of a comfortable home, good healthy food, a fine education and the chance to travel and gain knowledge of other people groups. All this can lend itself to a wealth of experience they can put to good use.

But "from everyone who has been given much, much will be demanded" (Luke 12:48). We are blessed so we can bless others; we are saved from sin's ravages and results so we can share with others that there is a way of peace and forgiveness. We are to serve God in our place, in our time. The gifts He gives us are to be held lightly and not tightly, and in the end we shall be held accountable for our stewardship. We can gift our children by our gifts or spoil our children with too much "stuff." Part of Job's heritage for all his children was to give them an example of benevolence and philanthropy so that they would follow in his steps. Being a good model is one of the best things any parent can leave behind. One of the most wonderful memories Job's children must have had of their father was of his faithfulness—his dignity as he handled misfortune and his resolute determination to do or say nothing that would reflect negatively on the Lord he worshiped and served.

The Heritage of Leadership

In chapter 29 of Job, we get a glimpse of Job's life when the "hedge" had been in place. It is a picture of a busy life in public service as he went to the gate of the city and took his seat in the public square. The leaders of his community, the chief men and nobles, and the young men spoke well of his judgment and leadership. But of what did Job's work, for which he was so highly thought of, consist?

It involved social concerns, practical assistance for the poor. He was a father to the orphans, a help to the dying, and he "made the widow's heart sing!" He was a justice of the peace, protecting the victim and meting out just punishment to those who exploited strangers. He had the wisdom of Solomon. "Men listened to me expectantly, waiting in silence for my counsel. After I had spoken, they spoke no more; my words fell gently on their ears. They waited for me as for showers and drank in my words as the spring rain" (Job 29:21–23).

Job was a man of his culture and time, a man for all seasons. He was serving God as best he knew how, using all his many gifts and abilities and spiritual wisdom for the good of the community. And what of chapter 42? What about the sons and daughters born after the death of his other children? Part of their inheritance would surely be to take the places of leadership their father, chief and king, left to them. Now Job was growing old, and it would be time to put his children into place as princes and princesses in their clan.

Perhaps Keren-Happuch inherited her father's great heart for the poor. Keren's name means "horn of antimony." This horn was used to mix a black powder into eye paint to enhance the beauty of a woman's eyes. The original mascara perhaps. In a culture where names mean so much, I have often wondered about this one! Why did Job name his third daughter Keren-Happuch? Was it because from her infancy she had gorgeous, black eyelashes that didn't need such black paint? It's a poor rose that needs painting, so they say! Perhaps the dark smudges of lashes enhancing her legendary beauty brought such a name to mind.

A woman's eyes were regarded as an important component of beauty in Job's day. Maybe God had amply gifted this beautiful baby girl with all the qualities sought after and admired by her generation. She may have been one who needed no help from the "horn," since nature had amply endowed her with her own natural enhancements.

Keren may also have been particularly gifted with the beautiful eyes of love and mercy. Perhaps working as the Proverbs 31 woman—reaching out her hand to the poor and needy, her heart broken, weeping with those that wept—she would not have had to worry about her mascara running!

It's amazing how God gifts us with all the equipment we need to do the work He has prepared for us to do! Even our physical makeup matches the tasks He has designed for us.

Psalm 139 says that God knit us together in our mother's womb. For what reason? That all the days ordained for us, written in His book, may be lived for Him and for His glory (139:16).

As I think about my own heritage, planned first of all by my heavenly Father and brought into being with the help of my earthly father, I marvel at the way He "embroidered" me in my mother's womb. I was made an English lady, painted with the colors of my culture. My very Britishness has given me a platform I never dreamed possible. My physical, mental and social makeup, my training and environment, prepared me for the ministry God had for me. He matched my background and gifts—and all that has gone into making me—with a needy world. All I needed was an encounter with God and a sense of responsibility and calling that went along with the God-given privileges of my life! Above all, He gave my heart the great desire to be one of Job's daughters.

And what of Jemimah? What of the eldest daughter mentioned here in Scripture? Jemimah (Yem-ee-maw) means "day by day." It has the sense in Hebrew of long-lastingness—of distance, perhaps of "going the distance." Maybe Job, looking back on his horrendous experience, wanted to capture one of the most meaningful lessons he had learned—that you can only go the distance "day by day," one step at a time.

Knowing God, Day by Day

As I write this chapter at the Wycliffe missionary conference, there are many Jobs here with us. There are also many of his daughters. It has not been hard to find one of them to illustrate the meaning of Jemimah's name. Sue Graham agreed to sit down with me and tell me her story.

Sue and Al Graham and their children translated the Bible into the heart language of a tribe in the jungles of Brazil. It took them twenty-six years to do it. Most of their weeks in the early days seemed to be filled with storms. In 1960 they persuaded a man to take them upriver to the village where they planned to work, but they met an Indian with a painted face, and the man was petrified and refused to take them any farther. So he let the family out on the first bank they came to! That was their initiation.

Their daughter Keren became sick with hepatitis, but they didn't realize what it was and continued their journey till they reached their destination. One of the natives who began to help them with the language was a witch doctor who, not surprisingly, proved deceitful in the information—the words—he was giving the missionaries. A few weeks later all but one of the family had hepatitis, and they ran out of all their medicines. The Indians would come by daily with such comforting words as "My uncle had that disease, and he died!" Fortunately they only discovered that later when they had learned the language! The Lord rescued them with a visit from some surveyors, who brought them mail.

They recouped in a missionary home in a small town, and as Sue lay in bed, she could see five vultures sitting on the roof of the next building.

"I remember being really depressed," she said, "and saying to Al, 'They're just waiting for me to die!' But I think the thing that kept me going and the thing the Lord gave me was that He had called me, that these people needed God's Word, and He had chosen us to do it. That's what brought me through even when I felt so low. I knew within my heart He was going to take us back."

And take them back He did. Their story is amazing. The chiefs said that their children could not play at the river because there were spirits at the water, and if they saw children playing, they would make everyone in the village sick. The same taboo pertained to the forest! So where were growing, lively kids to play? "The culture clashed with ours," Sue explained, "and there were cruel customs, such as an 'ant dance' where three or four hundred stinging ants were put in a glove, and the one who wore it longest would have good hunting!" The Grahams learned to respect what they could about the culture; they learned the language; they suffered isolation, loss of health and nearly loss of life. They kept on keeping on.

Sue Graham and her family are a family of Jobs; they raised five children in an unbelievable environment. One had just written to Sue, and she told me she had said, "Mom, it must be a special blessing for you to see every one of your children involved in the Lord's work." (Even though there were many difficult times in the children's search for their own identity and calling, four of them are going on to be missionaries.) With their translation finished, the Grahams are beginning to enjoy the blessings of Job 42. They are still working in their beloved Brazil. Sue Graham has learned to always abound in the work of the Lord, by the power of the Spirit, moment by moment, day by day.

What Does It Mean?

1. Discuss or write about the unusual thing Job did by giving his daughters an inheritance with their brothers. What does this action of one of God's favorite people say to women?

2. Discuss this statement with your group, or write about it in your journal or notebook: "A man of quality is never threatened by a woman of equality."

3. Jesus honored women. They were first at His birth, last at His tomb, and first to be given the news of Jesus' resurrection to share. Read Luke 8:1–3. What do these verses say about the "spiritual inheritance" Jesus gave to women of His day? What spiritual inheritance do you think Jesus gives women now?

4. If you are a woman, share or reflect in writing upon a time when God encouraged you through a man.

5. Discuss or write about the names of Job's daughters. Which one do you appreciate most and why?

6. Take each of Job's daughters' names—Jemimah, Keziah, and Keren-Happuch—and share the lesson you learned from each, verbally or in writing.

How Should I Pray?

Think of women you know who reflect the names of Job's daughters. Pray for:

- your own daughters, granddaughters, and other people's daughters you know

- oppressed women around the world
- the church—that it will encourage women to be all God meant them to be
- the women in your church and those who lead them.

Chapter Fifteen

FINISHING STRONG

And so he died, old and full of years.

Job 42:17

He who dwells in the shelter of the Most High
will rest in the shadow of the Almighty. . . .
"He will call upon me [God], and I will answer him;
I will be with him in trouble,
I will deliver him and honor him.
With long life will I satisfy him
and show him my salvation."

Psalm 91:1, 15–16

HOW old was Job when he died? Well over 140 years! That's old! He was a great-great-great-grandfather! That's a lot of fathering! "He saw his children and their children to the fourth generation" (Job 42:16). That's a lot of grandchildren! Job packed an awful lot of living and an awful lot of dying into his life. He lived a full life. It was full of joy and full of sorrow, full of peace and full of turmoil. It was full of desires realized and plans frustrated. Above all, it was "full of years."

Full of Years

The promise of a long life went along with God's promise of blessing. Many years were considered by the patriarchs to be a sign of God's benevolence. When God made a covenant with Abraham and promised him a son, He also promised him,

"You, however, will go to your fathers in peace and be buried at a good old age" (Gen. 15:15). Abraham, true to God's word (for it is God who numbers our days—Ps. 139:16), lived 175 years. "Then Abraham breathed his last and died at a good old age, an old man and full of years; and he was gathered to his people" (Gen. 25:8). I love that phrase "gathered to his people"—it sort of reassures me that I will see the family again!

When Joseph's brothers came to Egypt to ask for food during the famine, he eventually revealed his identity and forgave them for trying to kill him as a young boy, saying, "You intended to harm me, but God intended it for good." He sent his brothers back to bring his father, Jacob, now full of years, to Egypt. The night before Jacob took the long journey into Egypt, he was afraid. God came to him in a vision and told him not to be afraid to go because God would make of him a great nation and "Joseph's own hand will close your eyes," signifying his passing.

When the family arrived, Joseph presented his father to Pharaoh. The first question that Pharaoh asked was, "How old are you?" Jacob replied, "The years of my pilgrimage are a hundred and thirty. My years have been few and difficult, and they do not equal the years of the pilgrimage of my fathers." The Bible tells us that Jacob then blessed Pharaoh (47:8–10).

Pharaoh lived in Egypt, where the life expectancy of that time was twenty years! They considered that their gods smiled on anyone who made it out of their twenties and into their thirties. No wonder Pharaoh accepted Jacob's blessing! Here was a man from a tribe of men with longevity, which proved the grace and goodness of their God.

FINISHING STRONG

God is the giver of life. He holds our breath in His hands. And yet it is not how many years He gifts us with that matters in the end—it is what we do with those precious moments. It's not, after all, how a person begins life that heaven takes account of, but rather how he or she ends it! Finishing strong is so important. Job finished strong. Will we?

The Bible says, "Moses was a hundred and twenty years old when he died, yet his eyes were not weak nor his strength gone" (Deut. 34:7). He finished strong. When Joshua was in charge of possessing the land of Canaan, Caleb came to him and said, "I am . . . eighty-five years old! I am still as strong today as the day Moses sent me out; I'm just as vigorous to go out to battle now as I was then. Now give me this hill country that the LORD promised me that day" (Josh. 14:10–12). Caleb was a man, we are told, who "wholly followed the LORD" (14:8), and we see him finishing strong.

Others of God's best finished strong too; Gideon "died at a good old age" after having brought forty years of peace to the land in his service as a judge (Judg. 8:28–32). From David we hear testimony to the fact that

> He who dwells in the shelter of the Most High
>   will rest in the shadow of the Almighty. . . .
> "He will call upon me [God], and I will answer him;
>   I will be with him in trouble,
>   I will deliver him and honor him.
> With long life will I satisfy him
>   and show him my salvation." (Ps. 91:1, 15–16)

Solomon tells us that when we live in the fear of the Lord, God promises, "Through me your days will be many, and years will be added to your life" (Prov. 9:11). And this from a man who was given many, many years to fear the Lord but who blew it in the end!

Solomon did not finish strong. His wives stole his heart away from God, and he dishonored the name of the Lord. It is a fact that even though Solomon's God-given wisdom exceeded all the wisdom in the known world, he is known best for his one thousand wives and the excesses he allowed to corrupt his heart. How sad! Indeed, it's not how a person starts one's faith life that matters; it's how he or she finishes it.

WHAT MAKES LIFE FULFILLING?

If God gives us a life "full" of years, what will we fill them with? Will it be said of us, as it was said of King David, "When [he] had served God's purpose in his own generation, he fell asleep" (Acts 13:36)? Will they say that about our children and their children and their children after them? I surely hope so. "But," you may ask, "if my years are to be full, how do I fill them and with what?"

Integrity

First of all, make sure your life is full of integrity. Integrity means "soundness"—a strict, personal honesty with yourself and others. A healthy person is one who integrates principles into his life that give him wholeness. He makes sure he grows physically, emotionally, socially and spiritually. Job grew as a man in favor with God and man, in stature and wisdom, even as the prophet Samuel grew (1 Sam. 2:26), and later as did the Lord Jesus Himself. Job finished strong in the matter of integrity. In stark contrast King Solomon lost his integrity. He couldn't hold together what he professed spiritually with how he performed sensually. He didn't integrate his belief and behavior.

If we are going to finish strong, we have to keep a close watch on this. We have to be honest. We have to take notice of the devil's suggestions and refuse to give him a foothold. We need to sing with full intention:

Throw light into the darkened cells,
Where passion reigns within;
Quicken my conscience till it feels
The loathsomeness of sin.
                    —Frank Bottome

We need to keep on keeping on living transparently before God. Stuart and I were at a conference for leaders, and I noticed a seminar on "How to Affair-Proof Your Marriage." I was astounded. "Why do we need such a workshop at a conference like this?" I asked.

"Because of the moral failure of so many ministry leaders," I was told.

"Do you think such a seminar is necessary?" I asked a psychologist friend.

"Jill, it wouldn't be necessary if we were just honest with ourselves," he replied. "If we were honest with our own wayward nature and called ourselves to task. If we called flirting 'flirting' and refused to do it; if we acknowledged our quickened pulse when an attractive member of the opposite sex came around and flew to God in our minds; if we continually integrated our beliefs into our actions—then we wouldn't need seminars like this!" Job finished strong in the matter of integrity. I want to do the same.

Love

We see in Job's life story that he was motivated by the love of God. This *hesed* love is a love of decision rather than emotion. It is a determination to be primarily concerned with the well-being of another, whatever their response to us. Job did not run out of love for those he loved. In Romans 5:8 Paul tells us that God's love never fails to go on loving, even when nobody loves back. Job's human love was ruled and fueled by God Himself, and that is why we see him at the end of his life surrounded by his loved ones—although to love another is not a guarantee of being loved in return. He was old and full of years, yes, but he was also full of love.

I think of a modern-day Job, a friend and model in this regard. Robertson McQuilkin, president emeritus of Columbia International University, came to terms with his wife's Alzheimer's. He wrote of his experiences, saying such things as "She is such a delight to me. I don't 'have' to care for her—I 'get' to!" and "Had I not promised forty-two years before, 'in sickness and in health—till death do us part'? This was no grim duty to which I stoically resigned, however. It was only fair. She had, after all, cared for me for almost four decades with marvelous devotion—now it was my turn!" Robertson resigned as president of the Bible school and seminary in order to care for his wife. He is full of years, full of integrity and full of love! This is his prayer:

LET ME GET HOME BEFORE DARK

It's sundown, Lord.
The shadows of my life stretch back
into the dimness of the years long spent.
I fear not death, for that grim foe betrays himself at last,
thrusting me forever into life:
Life with you, unsoiled and free.
But I do fear.
I fear the Dark Spectre may come too soon—
or do I mean, too late?
That I should end before I finish or
finish, but not well.
That I should stain your honor, shame your name,
grieve your loving heart.
Few, they tell me, finish well . . .
Lord, let me get home before dark.
The darkness of a spirit
grown mean and small, fruit shriveled on the vine,

bitter to the taste of my companions,
burden to be borne by those brave few who
love me still.
No, Lord. Let the fruit grow lush and sweet,
a joy to all who taste;
Spirit-sign of God at work,
stronger, fuller, brighter at the end.
Lord, let me get home before dark.
The darkness of tattered gifts,
rust-locked, half-spent or ill-spent,
A life that once was used of God
now set aside.
Grief for glories gone or
fretting for a task God never gave.
Mourning in the hollow chambers of memory,
gazing on the faded banners of victories long gone.
Cannot I run well unto the end?
Lord, let me get home before dark.
The outer me decays—
I do not fret or ask reprieve.
The ebbing strength but weans me from mother earth
and grows me up for heaven.
I do not cling to shadows cast by immortality.
I do not patch the scaffold lent to build the real, eternal me.
I do not clutch about me my cocoon,
vainly struggling to hold hostage
a free spirit pressing to he born.
But will I reach the gate
in lingering pain, body distorted, grotesque?
Or will it be a mind
wandering untethered among light
phantasies or grim terrors?
Of your grace, Father, I humbly ask . . .
Let me get home before dark.

Robertson McQuilkin is finishing strong.

Hope

Third, our lives cannot be full if we do not have hope. Hope is one ingredient—along with love and faith—that sets God's people apart from the rest. We have every reason to be a hopeful people.

When you are 140 years old or more, you might not think there is much hope for a future at all. But Job exhibited his hope through such statements as, "After my skin has been destroyed, yet in my flesh I will see God" (19:26). That is the glorious hope of every believer.

Job had asked the rhetorical, "If a man dies, will he live again? All the days of my hard service I will wait for my renewal to come. You will call and I will answer you; you will long for the creature your hands have made. Surely then you will count my steps but not keep track of my sin" (14:14–16). Job used a military term, hard service. He talked about his renewal or his new assignment when forgiven and with the Lord—this Lord who created him longs for him. He loves and desires Job to come "home." Job looked forward to an eternity full of endless years! He knew that his Redeemer lived, and he also knew that he would live! He too wanted to "get home before dark"—the darkness of betraying his God or falling short of all God had for him to do.

The word meaning "hope" in the New Testament is *elpizo*. Paul uses it in First Corinthians 13:7 and says that love "always hopes." The believer recognizes the pain and present triumph of sin, but he cherishes the hope for the future victory of God.

The ancient Greeks had a fable about hope. They believed that hope was essential for the well-being of humankind. They said that Zeus gave humanity all good things in a basket. Curiosity, however, lifted the lid, and all the good things escaped back to the gods. The gods slammed the lid shut tight, and only hope was trapped, because the gods knew that hope was essential for our well-being. Our modern doctors and philosophers and psychiatrists would agree with the ancient Greeks. "Hope is essential for life," they say. "Where there is life, there's hope," the familiar saying goes. Actually, where there is hope, there is life!

Chapter 42 gives us a happy earthly ending to the story of Job. I love happy endings, don't you? But everyone's story doesn't end happily on earth. The good news for the Christian, however, is that every believer's story is not fully ended until we die—until, as Job puts it, our "renewal" comes. There is a chapter 42 for every single one of us! That is the final hope the Bible speaks about—the hope of heaven.

What can we hope for when the last chapter is written? We can look for the Lord's blessing in ways we have never, ever experienced it before. Job 42:12 says, "The LORD blessed the latter part of Job's life more than the first." We are told that he had fourteen thousand sheep, six thousand camels, one thousand yoke of oxen and one thousand donkeys. If you look in chapter one, that's double everything he had before. What a picture of heaven! Double the blessing and double the joy of anything here, however good we've had it. Everything we need, with double the capacity to enjoy it!

There will be many who do not have their earthly goods returned, who do not regain their health and strength down here or who are so broken in spirit they may never climb up out of the Slough of Despond to spiritual heights in this life. But we can hope that one day the last chapter will be written, and a new day will dawn for these people too.

Another exciting concept of heaven is the promise of comfort and consolation once we arrive home. Hope looks to the final victory of Jesus Christ—to the promise He gives of His final triumph over all that hurts and kills. Hope in the Christian's experience means we are sure of these things as we face the rest of our life down here and the rest of our life up there! We have hope in the sustaining power of God to help us to cope, to deal with the rest of the story, to keep hoping to the end and beyond to the realization of all our dreams. The hope of such consolation can keep us going! There are certainly ways we can comfort and console each other in the body of Christ. While we are still on this planet, there are touches of God's renewing and perfect healing of mind, body and spirit that must wait till the book of our life is closed forever and the glorious sequel—the second edition—is opened forever!

Looking Forward to the Lord's "Well Done"

Some veteran missionaries were returning to England for their retirement. They came by sea and enjoyed the long journey home. They were a little fearful of returning after more than forty faithful years of service on the foreign field, but they were excited about the people who would be there to meet the boat and the happy celebration and reunions that lay ahead. They were actually returning to the very same dockyard from which they had departed, and the thought of some of the missionary leaders in the delegation waiting to greet them and show appreciation for their long years of service together gave them a sense of sweet anticipation. As the boat came closer, it stopped to pick up some important people—public dignitaries or something of the sort.

When the boat finally edged its way into its dock, the two old servants of God leaned on the railing of the ship, scanning the faces in the waiting crowd for a familiar one. There was a lot of pomp and circumstance and happy noise as the red carpet was rolled out for the dignitaries on board. The band began to play, and flags began to wave. Cheers filled the air, and still, the two soldiers of the faith searched the sea of faces for their friends. There wasn't a sign of even one of them.

The "important" people had gone now. The band was packing up, and most of the people had claimed their passengers and left. The old couple looked at each other. "What a homecoming," said the wife, tears starting to come. They held each other tightly, eyes shut, arms around each other. And then the Lord said something! Yes, He did. Quietly but insistently, in both of their hearts, He whispered, "You're not home yet!" They opened their eyes, looked at each other and voiced them—the wonderful, whispered words! In unison they said, "But we're not home yet!"

One day the band would be playing, the angels would roll out the heavenly red carpet, flags would be flying, and the great crowd of witnesses in heaven, who had been watching them finish strong, would be singing, "Welcome home, children!" One day— but not yet. Yes, there had been a bad mistake by the mission in mixing up the time of their arrival, but the old couple knew there would be no such mistake one day! One day they would arrive in Job 42, and in no uncertain way, in the fullest sense! Then they would receive double for all their sacrifice of love.

At the end of the story, Job is restored to full health and vigor, honored and appreciated by everyone. God's Word tells us that if we finish strong, we will win the greatest honor of all. We will hear the Lord welcome us home with a great "Well done, good and faithful servant!" (Matt. 25:21). I want to strive for that prize, don't you? I don't want to hear the Lord say to me, "underdone" or "half-done" or "not done at all, you slothful servant!" One thing we can be sure about is this: If no one ever thanks us here, we will hear it up there—if we finish strong.

Job—full of years, full of integrity, love, and hope—hoped on to his end, which was really his beginning. Job, at the end of his life, had only just begun!

When Job Blesses Us

I had a dear friend who, on this earth, lived in a beautiful body. She had a vivacious personality and was an artist who painted all sorts of created things, particularly roses. I remember (will I ever forget?) the day she told me the doctors had diagnosed cancer. I watched in wonder as she descended onto her ash heap. At first she struggled because she couldn't sense God near, but then her faith took flight, and she began to testify to His saving and redeeming power in her life. Isaiah 63:9 became a favorite verse: "In all their distress he too was distressed, and the angel of his presence saved them. In his love and mercy he redeemed them; he lifted them up and carried them all the days of old." As Gleason Archer says, "Often through our heartaches, God brings about our greatest good and his greatest glory." And so it was with Carmen. She was able to believe the messenger— the doctor who, in the end after a brave battle, gave her two weeks to live. She gathered her large extended family around her. In those last weeks of her life, she began to encourage others. Like Job, she prayed for her friends. Like Job, she said, "My ears had heard of you but now my eyes have seen you. Therefore I despise myself and repent in dust and ashes" (42:5–6). This was not the ash heap of her dreams but the ash heap of humility born of a knowledge of God, who gave her dying grace. She was one of Job's most beautiful daughters.

She began to talk of "the great day." We realized she was talking about her death. She longed for her "renewal" as Job longed for his. She struggled to the last to finish some unfinished artwork, and when her great day came, her loved ones gathered up her paintings and decorated the church with them for the memorial service. A most beautiful rose on a huge canvas was set up in the front of the sanctuary by the pulpit. The day she knew she was on her final lap, she asked my husband to conduct her funeral and me to write a poem for it and read it. I looked at her, dumbstruck. She had been my Job, but now had become my Elihu! Here she was encouraging me to use the opportunity of her funeral service to encourage others even in my great grief at her passing. How could I say no? But how could I say yes? What would I say? During a long, sleepless night, I asked God to give me a song to sing—be it in a minor key! He did, and He gave me help through my tears (tears of joy for her, of sorrow for me) to give it.

To Carmen Collins

Greatest God and Heavenly Artist,
See our sense of loss and grief.
Speak a word of heavenly comfort,
Bring a breath of sweet relief.
On the canvas of our memories
Framed o'er thoughts of years past,
Dip Your brush in "Carmen Colours"
Paint a portrait that will last.
Picture of a cherished mother
Precious daughter, wife and friend,
Aunt and mentor, Jesus lover
He her Master, Saviour, Friend!
Tears are over, grief forgotten,
Joy now swells and fills her soul.
Loving God defuses anguish,
Body, soul and mind makes whole.
Carmen new dimension living
Purposeful existence knows,
Seeing God prepare His palette
Watching Jesus paint a rose.
Brushing sunsets with lights, colours
Misting meadows with His breath,
Praising Him in exultation

Carmen laughs with God at death!
Precious dear one missed already
As your loved ones mourn your loss,
May your death be our reminder
We can join you through His Cross.
Door to life Christ's rich atonement
Gift of love His tomb displays,
Cost God's Son His death to open
Heaven's joy to one who prays.
On the canvas of our memories Framed,
Oh God, o'er years to be,
Dip your brush in "Carmen Colours"
Paint a picture just for me.
Carmen vibrant life enjoying
Perfect health and wholeness knows,
Watches God prepare His colours
Helps her Jesus paint a rose!
                    —Jill Briscoe

Didn't Jesus say, "He who believes in me will live, even though he dies; and whoever lives and believes in me will never die" (John 11:25–26)? What a hope!

For Carmen it was glory; a new place and a new face—the very face of God—to praise. For Carmen it was Job chapter 42. It was her Great Day that would never end. For Carmen it was a "wooing" from the jaws of distress, to a spacious place free from restrictions (her oxygen tank and tubes), to the comfort of her table laden with food, as she feasted with her beloved Savior, who had come and carried her home. For Carmen, it was a new body; for "in her flesh," she saw God. And for us who were so glad, yet so sad, there was work to be done. There was, we knew too well, a world of Jobs out there—Jobs who needed an Elihu to encourage them, that they, in turn, might encourage us!

The "Job 42" chapter of Revelation tells us that one day "He will wipe away all tears from their eyes, and there shall be no more death, nor sorrow, nor crying, nor pain. All of that has gone forever" (Rev. 21:4, TLB).

Just imagine (though our tiny, finite minds find it almost impossible), no more funerals, no more caskets, no more graves, no more choked sobs, no more medicine, no more hospices, no more tubes and life-support systems, no more pain! No more headaches, stomachaches, backaches and heartaches! No more tears, no more wet pillows or dry-eyed grief that wants to cry and can't. No more little children with gaunt, skeletal figures staggering across our TV screens, drinking putrid water where the buzzards wait. No more husbands' throats slit in front of terrorized wives and children. No more killing fields, gas chambers, or genocide. No more burying people alive, crucifixion or torture chambers. No more famine, no more, no more, no more!

Only comfort, love, consolation and healing streams of grace. Only living water, the sunshine of God's face; only life, liberty; only angels and perfected Jesus-like people to join in laughter, love and praises to our God. Only worship, only praise, only total happiness and fulfillment—ONLY GOD! Only chapter 42! What a hope! And all for the asking.

Personal Application and Meditation

1. Spend time rereading key passages of Job, particularly chapters 1, 2, 3, 19 and 42.

2. What are the main encouragements you have gleaned from this book?

3. What will you say when someone asks you why God allows suffering?

4. How can you plan to "finish strong"?

5. Read Revelation 21–22. How do these chapters encourage you?

A Prayer to Make Your Own

Father, I come to You because You have invited me to. I understand Jesus made it possible for me to come into Your presence by giving Himself for me on the cross. I believe there is no other way for people to be forgiven. Please forgive my sins, and send Your Holy Spirit into my heart that I may have Your presence in my life, Your power in my weakness and Your peace in my pain.

Whether You allow me to live in chapter 1 of Job or chapter 42, keep me full of faith in Your provision for my needs, however great or small. May I speak well of You when trouble comes, and please bless me with a supportive family and friends—and an Elihu to help me stay focused on You. And make me a blessing, Lord. May others see me living a Resurrection faith in every storm of my life, even the darkest of storms that may be ahead. Thank You for giving Your Son, who died to make me ready for heaven and rose again to make me ready for earth. In Christ's name and victory, amen.

Name _____

Date _____

NOTES

Chapter 2

1. Morris A. Inch, *My Servant Job* (Grand Rapids: Baker Book House, 1979), preface.

2. Henry Gariepy, *Portraits of Perseverance* (Wheaton, IL: Victor Books, 1991), 45.

Chapter 3

1. David McKenna, *The Whisper of His Grace* (Waco, TX: Word, 1987), 25–27.

2. Elisabeth Elliot, *A Path Through Suffering* (Ventura, CA: Gospel Light, 2003), 13.

Chapter 4

1. Gariepy, 83.

Chapter 5

1. McKenna, 96–97.

Chapter 6

1. Warren Wiersbe, *The Bible Exposition Commentary/New Testament, Vol. 2* (Colorado Springs: David C. Cook, 2001), 193.

2. J.D. Douglas and Merrill C. Tenney, *NIV Compact Dictionary of the Bible* (Grand Rapids: Zondervan, 1999), 307.

3. Wiersbe, 193.

4. A.W. Tozer, *High Mountains, Deep Valleys* (Sutherland, Australia: Albatross Books, 1991), 350; quoting Arthur Helps.

Chapter 9

1. Joseph Scriven, "What a Friend We Have in Jesus" (1855).

Chapter 10

1. Chuck Swindoll, "Memorable Scenes," in *Old Testament Homes: Bible Study Guide* (Fullerton, CA: Insight for Living, 1992), 19.

Chapter 11

1. Ruth Bell Graham, *It's My Turn* (Old Tappan, NJ: Revell, 1982), 169.

2. C. Austin Miles, "In the Garden" (1912).

Chapter 12

1. McKenna, 43.

Chapter 13

1. David Augsburger, *The Freedom of Forgiveness* (Chicago: Moody Press, 1987), 16.

Chapter 14

1. Thomas O. Chisholm, William J. Kirkpatrick, "Oh, to Be Like Thee!"